Shot in a black-and-white palette of cigarette smoke, hair tonic, dark suits and pale button-down shirts, *Good Night, and Good Luck* plunges into a half-forgotten world in which television was new, the cold war was at its peak, and the Surgeon General's report on the dangers of tobacco was still a decade in the future. Though it is a meticulously detailed reconstruction of an era, the film, directed by George Clooney from a script he wrote with Grant Heslov, is concerned with more than nostalgia.

Burnishing the legend of Edward R. Murrow, the CBS newsman who in the 1940's and 50's established a standard of journalistic integrity his profession has scrambled to live up to ever since, *Good Night, and Good Luck* is a passionate, thoughtful essay on power, truth-telling and responsibility.

And be prepared to pay attention. *Good Night, and Good Luck* is not the kind of historical picture that dumbs down its material, or walks you carefully through events that may be unfamiliar. Instead, it unfolds, cinéma-vérité style, in the fast, sometimes frantic present tense, following Murrow and his colleagues as they deal with the petty annoyances and larger anxieties of news gathering at a moment of political turmoil. The story flashes back from a famous, cautionary speech that Murrow gave at an industry convention in 1958 to one of the most notable episodes in his career—his war of words and images with Senator Joseph R. McCarthy.

—A. O. Scott, *The New York Times*

# good night,
# and good luck.
## The Screenplay and History
## Behind the Landmark Movie

Screenplay Written by
George Clooney & Grant Heslov

Directed by
George Clooney

*Newmarket Press* *New York*

This book is published in the United States of America.

First Edition

10  9  8  7  6  5  4  3  2  1
ISBN-13: 978-1-55704-714-4 (pb)
ISBN-10: 1-55704-714-6 (pb)

Library of Congress Cataloging-in-Publication Data available upon request.

100866579X

QUANTITY PURCHASES
Companies, professional groups, clubs, and other organizations may qualify for special
terms when ordering quantities of this title. For information, write Special Sales Department, Newmarket Press, 18 East 48th Street, New York, NY 10017; call (212) 832-3575;
fax (212) 832-3629; or e-mail info@newmarketpress.com.

www.newmarketpress.com

Manufactured in the United States of America.

# Contents

# Preface

$G$*ood Night, and Good Luck* takes place during the early days of broadcast journalism in 1950s America. It chronicles the real-life conflict between television newsman Edward R. Murrow (David Strathairn) and Senator Joseph McCarthy and the Permanent Sub-committee on Investigations (Government Operations Committee). With a desire to report the facts and enlighten the public, Murrow and his dedicated staff—headed by his producer Fred Friendly (George Clooney) and Joe Wershba (Robert Downey Jr.) in the CBS newsroom—defy corporate and sponsorship pressures to examine the lies and scaremongering tactics perpetrated by McCarthy during his communist "witch-hunts." A very public feud develops when the senator responds by accusing the anchor of being a communist. In this climate of fear and reprisal, the CBS crew carries on regardless, and their tenacity eventually pays off when McCarthy is brought before the Senate and made powerless as his lies and bullying tactics are finally uncovered.

Directed by George Clooney, who co-wrote the script with the film's producer Grant Heslov, *Good Night, and Good Luck* stars David Strathairn as Murrow, Clooney as Fred Friendly, Robert Downey Jr. and Patricia Clarkson as Joe and Shirley Wershba, Frank Langella as Bill Paley, Ray Wise as Don Hollenbeck, Heslov as Don Hewitt, and Jeff Daniels as Sig Mickelson. Grammy® Award–winner Dianne Reeves appears and performs in the film as well.

A Section Eight, 2929 Entertainment, and Participant Productions production, *Good Night, and Good Luck* was executive-produced by Todd Wagner, Mark Cuban, Marc Butan, Steven Soderbergh, Jennifer Fox, Ben Cosgrove, Jeff Skoll, and Chris Salvaterra.

* * * *

The movie was released by Warner Independent Pictures in the United States on October 7, 2005, to wide critical acclaim, garnering numerous nominations and awards and inspiring a new interest in the period when Edward R. Murrow was broadcasting. The following articles, some written by the original participants, help give an overview of the historical events that have been captured so dramatically in *Good Night, and Good Luck.* Joe and Shirley Wershba, Ruth Friendly, Milo Radulovich, and Howard Weinberg deserve special thanks for their lively contributions and kind assistance in assembling this book.

We will not walk in fear, one of another. We will not be driven by fear into an age of unreason, if we dig deep in our history and our doctrine; and remember that we are not descended from fearful men. Not from men who feared to write, to speak, to associate, and to defend causes that were for the moment unpopular.

This is no time for men who oppose Senator McCarthy's methods to keep silent, or for those who approve. We can deny our heritage and our history, but we cannot escape responsibility for the result. There is no way for a citizen of a republic to abdicate his responsibilities. As a nation we have come into our full inheritance at a tender age. We proclaim ourselves, as indeed we are, the defenders of freedom, wherever it continues to exist in the world, but we cannot defend freedom abroad by deserting it at home. The actions of the junior Senator from Wisconsin have caused alarm and dismay amongst our allies abroad, and given considerable comfort to our enemies. And whose fault is that? Not really his. He didn't create this situation of fear; he merely exploited it—and rather successfully. Cassius was right. "The fault, dear Brutus, is not in our stars, but in ourselves." Good night, and good luck.

—Edward R. Murrow, *See It Now* broadcast, March 9, 1954

# Part One:
# The History

# The Night Television Documentaries Changed Forever

### by Fred W. Friendly

On October 20, 1953, *See It Now* broadcast "The Case Against Lt. Milo Radulovich." That night the face of television documentaries was changed forever.

At the time of the broadcast Senator Joseph McCarthy and his assault on individual rights had journeyed virtually unchecked into a third year. Although some had bravely stood their ground against the senator, none had slowed his pace. McCarthy was a bare-knuckled political brawler who basked in the headlines of shattered lives and destroyed careers. How ironic, then, that history would settle on a genteel physics student, a reserve Air Force weather officer, to deliver the first blow that could stagger Joe McCarthy.

Our program that Tuesday evening held up a mirror. For the first time Americans saw what McCarthyism had wrought. The Milo Radulovich program peeled back the wretched excess of Communist witch-hunts, and what we found startled us—a son who would not abandon his frightened, immigrant father; a student with a wife and two kids, working two jobs, and attending college under the GI bill; a reserve officer who had served his country with distinction for ten years and was being discharged from the military even though his

Foreword by Fred W. Friendly to *To Strike at a King: The Turning Point in the McCarthy Witch-Hunts,* by Michael Ranville (1997, Momentum Books, Troy, Michigan). Reprinted by kind permission of Ruth Friendly.

loyalty was not in question. Milo Radulovich was hardly the stuff of sedition.

I can still recall Murrow's impish grin as he thrust a *Detroit News* article my way during a chance meeting at an elevator. "Fritzl," he said—he was one of a select few who could get away with calling me that—"this could be the little picture for your McCarthy story."

"My McCarthy story," as he put it, referred to a question that was being asked of us almost daily that fall of 1953: when would Ed Murrow take on Joe McCarthy? Ed and I had discussed the matter in private many times. We agreed that when we did move there could be no margin for error, our story had to be directly on point. *See It Now* was built on a foundation of the "little picture," explaining a news event by showing the impact on one person. The McCarthy story had to be the *perfect* little picture. We were looking for a Milo Radulovich long before we knew who Milo was.

As time passed, Murrow's patience proved greater than mine. In private I began to push the matter. Ed's reticence, I suspect, could be traced to the questionable circumstances surrounding the death of his close friend Laurence Duggan five years earlier. But hesitation vanished when we found Milo.

There are many reasons why the Milo Radulovich program will always hold a special place in the hearts of our *See It Now* family. Milo was such an honest man, his story so compelling, that McCarthyites couldn't just dismiss this outrageous miscarriage of justice by hiding it behind a cloak of national security. The case of Milo Radulovich underscored that the hunt for witches had gone too far.

With benefit of hindsight, our March 1954 *See It Now* broadcast on Joe McCarthy has been credited with playing a key role in the senator's demise. There is no question that without "The Case Against Lt. Milo Radulovich" five months earlier, we never could have done the McCarthy program.

The Radulovich program will also be remembered for the role it played in shaping television documentaries. We had done stories on many of the day's pressing issues. We railed against juvenile delinquency. But who didn't abhor the wasting of lives at such an early age? We went to Korea and trained our cameras, not on the war, but on those who were fighting it. But whose heart didn't ache for a lonely GI in a combat zone away from home at Christmas? We were proud of those programs, and countless others, but to some extent when it came to conflict we were apostles of the obvious. Our program on Milo changed all that.

Despite numerous requests the Pentagon wouldn't comment on Milo's case. We were faced with what was looming to be the most controversial broadcast to date in the history of television, and telling only one side of the story. Murrow and I discussed our uneasiness and concluded that sometimes there just aren't arguments on both sides of an issue.

Our fondness for the Radulovich program also stemmed from the fact that it epitomized what we were all about at *See It Now*. It was controversial, but adrenaline at *See It Now* was the daily companion that kept our wits sharp. We had less than a week to put the program together, not an easy task in the 1953 world of television. But we learned to function with one eye fixed on a clock that went twice its normal speed the closer we got to our weekly rendezvous with 10:30

p.m. Tuesday. We believed in the little picture. And Milo Radulovich was the perfect little picture to illustrate the ravages of McCarthyism.

Milo is far more than a footnote to McCarthyism. He was a major participant, and a book on his role is long overdue. Ed Murrow and I maintained that the Radulovich program was one of the finest things we'd ever done, a rare moment in history. Four decades later I cannot quarrel with that assessment.

Of all the broadcasts I have been involved in, of all the issues I have examined, I select the Milo Radulovich program to show my students each semester at the Columbia School of Graduate Journalism. I have found no better way to illustrate the role journalism plays in a free and open society than by citing "The Case Against Lt. Milo Radulovich."

# The Man Who Fought McCarthy's Red Smear

## by Julie Morris

Milo Radulovich, 26, was a WWII veteran, finishing his education at the University of Michigan on the GI Bill. He was hoping to get a degree in physics so he could advance in his career as a meteorologist. He lived in Dexter, MI, with his wife Nancy and their two daughters. He was doing very well in his junior year and hoped to obtain a government job after school.

He had joined the Army Air Corps in 1944 and became a meteorologist. He was a first lieutenant when he was discharged in 1952. As a weather forecaster, he had top-secret clearance and was required to remain in the reserves. In September 1953 he received a letter informing him he was being dismissed from the reserves as a poor security risk because of his continued relationship with his father and sister who were deemed left-wing sympathizers.

The nation was caught in a "red scare" hysteria, whipped up by the junior Senator from Wisconsin, Joseph McCarthy. Milo's father, John, had immigrated to Detroit in 1914 from Serbia and was labeled a Communist because he subscribed to a pro-Communist paper from Serbia. The fact that he also subscribed to the anti-Communist paper was deemed irrelevant. The elder Radulovich didn't speak or read

From *The Detroit News* website (November 19, 2005). ©2005 by The Detroit News. Reprinted with permission. Julie Morris is a staff writer.

English well and subscribed to both Serbian-language newspapers to keep up on events in his native Serbia.

Milo's sister, Mrs. Margaret Fishman, was labeled a Communist because she had attended suspected Communist meetings and demonstrations. Milo Radulovich was guilty by association.

Few attorneys were willing to take on his case, fearing they themselves would be labeled as Communist sympathizers, but Milo was referred to Charles C. Lockwood, who had a reputation for representing underdogs. He took Milo's case without charge.

Lockwood convinced Milo to tell his story to *The Detroit News*. To their surprise the story was published on the front page the next day. An old Army and college buddy of Milo's—Attorney Kenneth Sanborn—saw the article and volunteered to help, also free of charge.

On Oct. 14, 1953, *The News* printed another front-page article on the case, and this time it attracted the attention of CBS newsman

*Milo Radulovich reads a letter of support as he sits with his wife, Nancy, and his two daughters, 1953.*

Edward R. Murrow in New York. Murrow hosted a television news-magazine show called *See It Now*, where he occasionally focused on what he called the "little picture." Murrow was anxious to expose Sen. McCarthy's anti-Communist witch-hunts and had been waiting for the right story of an average citizen being persecuted. When he read of Milo Radulovich he was certain he had found it.

Murrow took *The Detroit News* story to his CBS producer Fred Friendly. Friendly immediately dispatched reporter Joe Wershba to Dexter to interview Radulovich, his father and sister. Wershba called Friendly that evening and told him this was definitely the story they needed.

In the days prior to the broadcast of Murrow's show on Radulovich, CBS executives distanced themselves from it, fearing a backlash from the show's sponsor, Alcoa, which was a major U.S. Air Force supplier. Alcoa decided that it would drop its midshow commercial to avoid problems with the government.

As the Oct. 20 broadcast date approached CBS refused to advertise it in the media. Friendly and Murrow spent $1,500 of their own money to place an ad promoting the show in *The New York Times*. A nervous CBS demanded they pay cash in advance so the network would not be involved.

After the broadcast, calls began pouring into CBS from around the nation praising Murrow and the show. *The New York Times* television critic John Crosby described Murrow as "The St. George of Television." Oddly the program was not aired in Detroit by the local CBS affiliate.

The show was, according to Friendly, "the shortest half hour in the history of television." It consisted of filmed interviews with Milo, his wife, and father. CBS reporters had combed the town of Dexter looking for opposition to Milo but all supported his fight.

On Nov. 24, five weeks after the show aired, Harold E. Talbott, Secretary of the Air Force, reversed the findings of the administrative board of three Air Force colonels that had declared Radulovich a security risk. He was cleared of all charges.

It was the beginning of the end for Sen. McCarthy. Murrow aired an attack on McCarthy in March of 1954 and gave McCarthy a show of his own to respond. McCarthy's only response was to call Murrow a Communist.

Radulovich recounted the case 14 years later in a *Detroit News* interview with Richard Ryan, "There is absolutely no question that it affected my life. It stopped me from achieving some of the goals I wanted to attain. I never got my college degree and that bugs the hell out of me."

What Radulovich does remember with some pride, is that he may have contributed to bringing an end to the "red scare" period. "This compensates me for nearly everything I lost. There are probably a lot of guys floating around now washing garbage cans who were involved in the same period. And there might have been a lot more. I consider myself really lucky. It is only by the grace of public opinion that I was able to carry my fight. If it hadn't been for *The Detroit News* I don't know where I would be today. Where else but in this country can you find a free press that is willing to express itself to save a little man?"

Milo Radulovich eventually retired as a meteorologist for the National Weather Service and lives in Sacramento.

The following appeared in *The Detroit News* on Jan. 5, 1954, as a Letter to the Editor:

Your participation in the fight to vindicate our family from the attacks of an unknown enemy caused you, I am sure, to invest much of your professional time and talent toward our ultimate victory.

Your energetic efforts in our behalf aided the work of our attorneys, Charles C. Lockwood and Kenneth N. Sanborn, in bringing the truth to our governmental authorities in Washington.

Your fight in the case of my son, Milo Radulovich, and his family caused our people to take up the fight for complete vindication. The word "thank-you" is small indeed. We are happy and we hope that God will reward your efforts.

Happy 1954 to all of you.

—John Radulovich

# Murrow vs. McCarthy: See It Now
## by Joseph Wershba

O n a wall of Joseph McCarthy's Senate office there used to hang a framed quotation, its author unknown:

"Oh, God, don't let me weaken. Help me to continue on. And when I go down, let me go down like an oak tree felled by a wood-man's ax."

In its March 8, 1954, cover story, *Time* magazine took note of that prophetic inscription as it profiled the junior senator from Wisconsin, then at the very height of his political power. For four years he had terrorized the nation with his wild and exaggerated charges that nearly every branch of the government had been infiltrated by Communists and fellow travelers who were busily doing the Soviet Union's dirty work. In the cold-war climate of fear that the senator was exploiting and exacerbating, the careers of many eminent men and women were being destroyed on the basis of hearsay evidence—or no evidence at all—and McCarthy's rampage seemed unstoppable.

McCarthy had just humbled Secretary of the Army Robert Stevens in what was universally—and fearfully—described as "the Army's surrender to McCarthy." The Senate, in Walter Lippmann's words, "in order not to appear red, [had] decided to be yellow." And even the White House hesitated to give offense to the senator. "I'm not going to get down into the gutter with *that* guy," President Eisen-

Joseph Wershba wrote a book-length account of his experience in 1955, the year after the historic program aired. An edited version first appeared in *The New York Times Magazine* on March 4, 1979, to mark the broadcast's twenty-fifth anniversary. That version is reprinted here by kind permission of the author.

*Senator Joseph McCarthy covers a microphone while Roy Cohn talks
to him during a televised subcommittee meeting, April 23, 1954.*

hower had told his intimates—thus ensuring that the entire country
would be in the gutter with "that guy" for at least another year.

True, the Army was beginning to leak details of its long-awaited
"bill of particulars" against the senator, charging that McCarthy and
his chief counsel, Roy Cohn, had applied improper pressure in order
to obtain special advantages for a drafted member of their staff, Private G. David Schine, but *Time* noted the weakness of the army's case
and warned:

"The ax that will cut down McCarthy's power will have to be a lot
sharper than those in the hands of Stevens & Co. last week. That
mighty oak must be approached with caution; it is covered with *Toxi-
codendron radicans*, i.e., poison ivy."

It took more than one ax to topple Joe McCarthy, but next Friday
marks the twenty-fifth anniversary of one of the first and most deadly
blows. It fell on March 9, 1954, at 10:30 in the evening, Eastern

Standard Time, when Edward R. Murrow spoke out against the senator on his famous television program *See It Now.*

Three years later, shortly before his death from acute hepatitic failure—largely the result of acute alcoholism that had been aggravated by his political decline—Senator McCarthy sought out Murrow at a Washington party, threw his arm around his shoulder, and asked with a grin, "No hard feelings, Ed?" It was a hallmark of McCarthy's ambivalence that he rarely wished to hurt the people he tried to destroy—and of his blindness that he did not realize that Murrow's broadcast had signaled the beginning of the end of his career.

On November 17, 1953, F.B.I. Director J. Edgar Hoover was testifying before a Senate committee. I was covering the story with a camera crew for *See It Now* and was rushing out of the Senate Caucus Room to find a soundman when I was stopped short by Don Surine, a former F.B.I. agent and one of Senator McCarthy's most trusted investigators and closest confidants.

"Hey, Joe!" he said. "What's this Radwich junk you're putting out?"

His pronunciation was off, but his reference was clear. A month before, *See It Now* had done a story about Lieutenant Milo Radulovich, whom the Air Force had tried to force to resign because it suspected his father and sister of Communist sympathies. After the program caused a sensation, the Air Force cleared Radulovich and dropped the case.

I muttered hurriedly to Surine that I had no time to talk. His wide eyes caught fire. He placed his hand on my arm and said, "What would you say if I told you Murrow was on the Soviet payroll in 1934?"

I must have looked as stunned as I felt. "Come on up to the office," he said savagely. "I'll show you!" I followed him to the fourth floor, and when we arrived at Senator McCarthy's office, Surine told me to wait outside.

I waited and out he came with a photostat of a story from the *Pittsburgh Sun-Telegraph,* dated February 18, 1935. "American Professors, Trained by Soviet, Teach in U.S. Schools," read the headline.

It was a Hearst "exposé" of American educators connected with a
forthcoming seminar of American students at Moscow University.
Essentially an attack against George S. Counts, a well-known professor of education and an adviser to the Institute of International
Education, the story said that among those "tied up with Dr. Counts,
of Columbia University and Moscow, in his propaganda crusade...we
find the following names...." There followed a list of distinguished
educators, headed by John Dewey and including the presidents of
several of America's finest universities. Probably the most obscure
name at that time was that of Edward R. Murrow, then assistant director of the Institute of International Education, which organized
educational seminars in many countries and arranged the exchange of
students and faculty members. The burden of the article's charge was
that these educators were inveigling American youths to go to
Moscow University for the summer to become "adept COMMU-
NIST PROPAGANDISTS."

Still stunned by Surine's flat assertion that Murrow "was on the
Soviet payroll in 1934," I asked him how this nearly twenty-year-old
story backed up his charge. He explained that the institute's seminar
would have been conducted under the auspices of a Soviet cultural organization known as VOKS, which was actually an espionage agency.
Ironically, though neither Surine nor I knew it that day, the Moscow
seminar had never taken place; it had been canceled by the Soviet
government. But in 1953, the combination of the words "international," "education," "Moscow," and "Murrow" were grist for the
McCarthy mill. He had already devastated government agencies for
much less.

Surine must have sensed that he had overreached himself. But he
went on, if for no other reason than to warn Murrow through me that
McCarthy had been keeping an eye on him ever since the Radulovich
story, and that he'd better watch his step. "Mind you, Joe," he said almost gently. "I'm not saying Murrow is a Commie himself. But he's one
of those goddamn anti-anti-Communists, and they're just as dangerous. And let's face it. If it walks like a duck, talks like a duck, and acts
like a duck, then, goddammit, it *is* a duck!" This was standard taxonomy
in the McCarthy School of Political Zoology: guilt by association.

*Edward R. Murrow, January 1954*

Such guilt could be spread in any and all directions, as Surine's next remark made quite clear. "It's a terrible shame," he said, "Murrow's brother being a general in the Air Force...."

By now I had recovered somewhat. "I think you guys go too far," I said. "After all, you take Churchill's war memoirs [which were then being serialized in *The New York Times*]. Just the other day, Churchill seemed to be blaming Eisenhower for letting the Russians get to Berlin before we did during the war. Hell, you're not going to say that Eisenhower sold out, too?"

We were walking down the marble staircase at the end of the fourth floor, and Surine stopped me at midlanding. He looked at me very deliberately and said, "Joe, you will remember in the '52 campaign, we never gave a blank check in our support of Dwight Eisenhower's candidacy." The "we" meant McCarthy, although it would be another year before the senator publicly stretched his "twenty years of treason" charge against the Democrats to include the Eisenhower administration, and by that time he was politically finished.

I paid my final obeisances to Surine as we reached the third floor. "Don, can I have this photostat?"

"Sure."

"Do I have your permission to show it to Murrow?"

"Sure."

If Surine wanted to feel that he had thrown a scare into me, I gave him every reason to think so. My parting shot was a feeble jest: "Take it easy, Don. Just remember, this is my bread and butter you're playing with."

I saw Murrow the next evening in his New York office after his nightly radio broadcast. Weakened by a heavy cold, he looked pallid. I told him about my meeting with Surine and showed him the photostat. He reddened a bit, then a weak grin came to his face. "So, *that's* what they've got," he said softly.

I often played the court jester to Murrow, and I thought the gambit might be useful now. "Mr. Murrow, you've had a long and honorable career, enough to enable any man to retire to the role of country gentleman." A slight scowl crossed his face and he began to talk about the climate of fear that had blanketed the country in general and the communications industry in particular. "I haven't even been able to talk about the whole problem of relations with Communist China." It was the only time I had ever heard Murrow concede that the McCarthyism poisoning the soul of the nation had penetrated his soul, too. He seemed beat. But I was mistaking his illness for his reaction to McCarthy's smear.

The next day, Murrow came up to me. His cold and his pallor were gone. He drew his lips back and his large, uneven teeth looked ready to chomp a live bear. "The question now is, *When* do I go against these guys?" He was in a quiet rage and he would stay that way for the next four months. At that moment, at the water fountain on the seventeenth floor of CBS, I felt an involuntary sense of pity for Joe McCarthy.

For Murrow was, above all else, "a *fighting* man"—as Albert Einstein warmly greeted him after the McCarthy affair. Murrow once told an interviewer that while he had been a correspondent in Europe, he had watched entire nations surrender to Hitler without a fight, and that the one thing he could not abide was death without battle. And Murrow's *See It Now* broadcasts on civil-liberties questions—especially the Radulovich program—at a time when McCarthy's reign of terror held America in thrall made a clash between the two men almost inevitable.

Still, it was a fray that Murrow had been slow to enter. Other journalists—such as columnists Joseph and Stewart Alsop and political cartoonist Herblock—had been assailing McCarthy while Murrow had remained silent. Some of his colleagues worried that Murrow was resting on the laurels he had won as a wartime correspondent and was settling into the role of a celebrity—like the stars in whose homes he conducted awkward interviews on his other television show, *Person to Person*. Murrow was sensitive to the criticism of other reporters that he had turned from a newsman into a showman; at times he would talk about "getting out of the entertainment business." Perhaps his stung pride gave Murrow's attack on McCarthy, when it finally came, a sharper edge. But it was precisely the popularity of *Person to Person*, which had millions more viewers than *See It*

*Photo courtesy of Ruth Friendly*

*Fred Friendly and Edward R. Murrow in a screening room watching
footage for an episode of the television news documentary* See It Now.

*Now* could ever claim, that made Murrow's attack so powerful in
terms of reaching a broad-based audience. For it was inconceivable to
these starry-eyed millions that the commentator who had taken them
into the boudoirs of Hollywood sexpots could be anything but a true-
blue American.

The tactical command of Operation McCarthy was taken over by
the producer of *See It Now,* Fred W. Friendly. In fact, *See It Now was*
Fred Friendly just as much as it was Ed Murrow. Their association
had resulted in the famous *I Can Hear It Now* record albums, the
prize-winning *Hear It Now* radio documentaries and, finally, *See It
Now.* Friendly's feeling for Murrow was, frankly, hero worship, and
Murrow in turn was respectful but, on occasion, painfully patroniz-
ing. He had given Friendly the diminutive nickname of "Fritzl," and
Friendly winced every time he heard it. But Murrow admired
Friendly's talent and backed him to the hilt. Friendly, meanwhile,

brought out the best in Murrow and swung weight at CBS because he had Murrow's prestige to swing.

If anyone other than Murrow and Friendly had planned a program attacking Joe McCarthy, it probably would have been nixed by the CBS hierarchy. But their prestige was such that William S. Paley, chairman of the network, and Frank Stanton, its president, lent them tacit support—after all, without their approval the broadcast could never have been aired.

Nor did Friendly and Murrow run into any trouble with their sponsor, the Aluminum Company of America. A few years before, when Alcoa had agreed to sponsor *See It Now*, Murrow had met with executives of the powerful corporation. One of them asked him, "Tell me, Mr. Murrow, just what are your politics?"

"Gentlemen, that is none of your business," Murrow replied.

Far from being angered, the Alcoa executive reacted with an enthusiastic "I *knew* that would be your answer!" Alcoa was sold on Murrow then and there, and never tried to influence his program.

Still, during the preparation of the show there was one distressing moment when it seemed as if we were about to buckle under and play according to McCarthy's witch-hunting rules. Friendly assembled the staff and grimly warned that if anyone in the room felt he had any associations, past or present, that would hurt *See It Now* he should speak up. But before anyone even had a chance to respond, Friendly rushed ahead: "And I'll brain whoever says anything."

In later weeks, a few troubled colleagues approached Friendly to confide about potential problems in their pasts. Friendly was brusque: "Paley says he'll have no more of this guilt by association. We're not going to play McCarthy's game anymore." (Would that Friendly had been right. In one form or another, broadcasting's blacklisting system would persist for at least another decade.)

By Saturday, March 6, 1954, Friendly had whipped the McCarthy program into shape. Each week in February, Friendly's film editors had asked, "This week?" Friendly would then consult with Murrow and return with the word: "Nope, we hold for a week." Murrow was calling the signals and now the most important consideration had become timing. Each week's delay increased the risk that McCarthy might strike first with his twenty-year-old exposé.

On Sunday, Murrow, appropriately dressed in a hunter's shirt, stretched tensely on one of the soft leather armchairs in the *See It Now* projection room on Fifth Avenue. Friendly ran off the film clips that Murrow would work with when he took to the air. Murrow courteously inquired of the staff—reporters, film editors, projectionists, the office boy, everyone except Friendly—whether they thought the film would be effective. The reporters said no, the cutting staff said yes. Friendly said nothing. Earlier in the day, Murrow had phoned and told him to make ready the film. "Fred," Murrow had said, "I've been thinking over a lifetime and I've come to a decision." That had been enough for Friendly.

Murrow evinced an interest in why the reporters thought the film was weak. I repeated what some of the others felt: The film was neutral, simply a photographic record of McCarthy in action that, by itself, would merely reinforce the belief of the senator's supporters in his greatness. Public opinion polls were already registering a frightening increase in McCarthy's popularity. Murrow pointed to the darkened screen and said: "The terror is right here in this room."

Two of us asked what Murrow intended to say. He answered, "No one man can terrorize a whole nation, unless we are all his accomplices." He thought a moment and added, "If none of us ever read a book that was 'dangerous,' had a friend who was 'different,' or joined an organization that advocated 'change,' we would all be just the kind of people Joe McCarthy wants." It was the first and last time that Ed Murrow ever made an "ideological" preachment to his staff, and it created a profound silence.

After a while, I rose and said, "Mr. Murrow, it's been a privilege to have known you and worked for you."

There was a skipped beat of silence, then Friendly laughed and broke the spell: "Hey, what do you mean, '*have*'?"

I corrected myself: "It *is* a privilege to know you."

A woman film editor leaned forward and asked plaintively, "But isn't the White House ever going to do something about McCarthy?"

Murrow reddened and replied with harsh evenness: "The White House is not going to do, and not going to say, one goddamned thing." It was a measure of Murrow's intense conviction: He did not use profanity in the presence of women and rarely at other times.

After another pause, he brought the session to a formal end: "Ladies and gentlemen, thank you. We go with this Tuesday night."

Having announced his decision, Murrow's inner tension evaporated quickly. He reverted to his usual pleasantries and, once again, referred to Friendly as "Fritzl." It was a red flag in front of a bull, and this time Friendly reacted strongly. "Ed, if you only knew how distasteful I find that name...."

Murrow looked at Friendly's pained futures. "O.K., Fred," he apologized, aware that others besides himself were putting their futures on the line in the battle that was soon to be joined.

Friendly and I lived in the same housing development. As we shared a taxi home that night, he seemed deep in thought until suddenly he burst out, "Well, even if Ed winds up without a job after Tuesday night, we'll make him President of the United States yet!"

On Monday, March 8, Joseph McCarthy came lunging into New York, demanding equal time from CBS and NBC to answer a televised speech by Adlai Stevenson. The networks began to panic. But so, too, did the Republican National Committee. Chairman Leonard Hall and other party leaders were fearful that McCarthy would use the free air time not to assail Stevenson and the Democrats but to go after Eisenhower, as he had in a previous broadcast. They and the networks announced that Vice President Richard M. Nixon would reply to Stevenson's attack.

McCarthy was in a mounting fury as he wandered through New York's Television Canyon, followed by a horde of press. He was delegating no one to answer Stevenson's attacks on him, he said. When a reporter suggested that the networks were within their legal rights to turn the time over to Nixon, McCarthy snapped back ominously: "The networks will grant me time, or learn what the law is." He must have felt in his bones that something was going wrong.

On Tuesday, Friendly and I worked with Murrow in his office, putting the final script together. The usual procedure was for Friendly to write a script after the film had been cut. Murrow would then make a few changes, but generally he wound up with something close to Friendly's original. This time, however, Murrow took over completely, dictating every word. The atmosphere was incredibly tense, but if Murrow felt it, he didn't show it. He was the "public" Murrow in action—cold, reserved, seemingly even bored as he methodically reached for the relentless words that would hammer nails into McCarthy's political coffin. At one point he directed me to excerpt key lines from the editorials of the nation's newspapers. In February, many of them had reacted vigorously for the first time when McCarthy denounced Brigadier General Ralph Zwicker as "unfit to wear the uniform" because a dentist had been promoted to the rank of major even though he had refused to answer Army security questionnaires about his political affiliations. "Give me the short, active words," Murrow ordered. It was an indication of Murrow's literary debt to another public writer who liked "short, active words" —Winston Churchill.

At 9:30 that evening, the *See It Now* production crew was at battle stations for a rehearsal in the control room of Studio 41 on the third floor of the CBS television center in New York's Grand Central Terminal. Friendly, once again, was in complete command. He took his usual position, curled up on the floor of the cramped control room at Murrow's foot, and tapped it when Murrow's cue to talk came up.

Running through his script, Murrow was savage and contemptuous. He always sweated profusely from his chin, and he came out of rehearsal wiping his makeup. "Those lights in there are hot," he said. I answered that I thought it would be even hotter in millions of homes in a few minutes. It was.

The broadcast began calmly. "Good evening," Murrow said. "Tonight *See It Now* devotes its entire half-hour to a report on Senator Joseph R. McCarthy, told mainly in his own words and pictures. But first, Alcoa would like you to meet a man who has been with them for fifty years." The commercial, plodding and old-fashioned even then, ran for three minutes that seemed like the proverbial eternity.

Then it was Murrow's turn again: "Because a report on Senator McCarthy is by definition controversial, we want to say exactly what we mean to say, and I request your permission to read from the script...." Murrow was one of the few broadcasters who could read from a script, his head down, and yet in the moment he lifted his gaze, rivet his audience's attention.

"Our working thesis tonight is this question: 'If this fight against communism is made a fight against America's two great political parties, the American people know that one of these parties will be destroyed—and the republic cannot endure very long as a one-party system.'

"We applaud that statement, and we think Senator McCarthy ought to. He said it seventeen months ago in Milwaukee."

There followed a film clip of the senator delivering these lines. Then Murrow turned on a tape recorder set before him and the voice of McCarthy charged the Democrats with "twenty years of treason" and declared, "The hard fact is that those who wear the label 'Democrat' wear it with the stain of a historic betrayal."

Then to candidate Eisenhower, pledging to root out subversion from the executive branch if he was elected president, followed by McCarthy patronizing the general as a great American. But the senator warned that he would continue to "call them as I see them, regardless of who happened to be president"—and giggled breathlessly into the microphone.

Murrow charged that McCarthy, "often operating as a one-man committee, has traveled far, interviewed many, terrorized some, accused civilian and military leaders of the past administration of a great conspiracy to turn the country over to communism, investigated and substantially demoralized the present State Department...."

The senator was shown reading from the transcript of a hearing in which he had chastised an Army general for "protecting" Communists. His reading ended with a strangled cry. "And wait till you hear the bleeding hearts scream and cry about our methods...," he told a sympathetic audience as he brushed his hand through his sparse hair with a sarcastically effeminate gesture. "'Oh, it's all right to uncover [Communists], but don't get rough doing it, McCarthy.'"

Next came film of Army Secretary Stevens saying he would not allow his officers to be subjected to any more of McCarthy's browbeating, and of President Eisenhower issuing still another ambiguous statement about McCarthy—with the senator replying that opposition to him was being engineered by "the extreme left-wing elements of press and radio."

Murrow reached over to a pile of newspapers and read their editorial condemnations of McCarthy's bully-ragging of Army personnel. "McCarthy will better serve his cause if he learns to distinguish the role of investigator from the role of avenging angel"—this was from the *Chicago Tribune,* which ordinarily supported the senator.

Murrow then turned to McCarthy's style: the demagogy, the insinuations, the half-truths and utter falsehoods. "Alger—I mean, Adlai," the senator said, pretending to mistake Stevenson for Hiss and then trying to prove that Stevenson had been appointed the American representative to an international conference at Hiss's insistence. Murrow followed up McCarthy's charges, showing them to be groundless.

Similarly, Murrow examined a hearing in which the senator had not only smeared the witness—Reed Harris of the State Department's International Information Administration—but had also thrown in the American Civil Liberties Union for good measure as "having been listed as a front for—and doing the work of—the Communist party." In those days, "listing" meant having been added to the United States Attorney General's list of subversive organizations—a list that did not include the A.C.L.U., Murrow pointed out, adding that the A.C.L.U. had received letters of commendation from Presidents Eisenhower and Truman and General MacArthur. But Reed Harris had been forced to resign. (One of Murrow's first acts upon being appointed head of the United States Information Agency by President Kennedy in 1961 would be to hire Harris as his deputy.)

The broadcast showed McCarthy in many of his aspects—tough, tender, brutal to his opponents, apprehensive of enemies lying in wait. And Murrow completed the devastating portrait in his concluding remarks.

"No one familiar with the history of this country can deny that congressional committees are useful. It is necessary to investigate before legislating. But the line between investigation and persecuting is a very fine one, and the junior senator from Wisconsin has stepped over it repeatedly. His primary achievement has been in confusing the public mind between the internal and the external threat of communism. We must not confuse dissent with disloyalty. We must remember always that accusation is not proof and that conviction depends upon evidence and due process of law. We will not walk in fear, one of another. We will not be driven by fear into an age of unreason if we dig deep in our history and our doctrine and remember that we are not descended from fearful men, not from men who feared to write, to speak, to associate, and to defend causes which were, for the moment, unpopular.

"This is no time for men who oppose Senator McCarthy's methods to keep silent—or for those who approve. We can deny our heritage and our history, but we cannot escape responsibility for the result.... We proclaim ourselves, as indeed we are, the defenders of freedom—what's left of it—but we cannot defend freedom abroad by deserting it at home. The actions of the junior senator from Wisconsin have caused alarm and dismay amongst our allies abroad and given considerable comfort to our enemies. And whose fault is that? Not really his. He didn't create this situation of fear. He merely exploited it, and rather successfully. Cassius was right: 'The fault, dear Brutus, is not in our stars, but in ourselves.'

"Good night, and good luck."

The broadcast concluded, the country responded. CBS said it was the greatest spontaneous response in the history of broadcasting: 12,348 telephone calls and telegrams in the first few hours. According to the network, 11,567 of these supported Murrow. (Today the CBS vaults contain 22 boxes, each containing between 750 and 1,000 communications. Eighteen are marked "Favorable," and the remaining four, "Unfavorable.")

We waited long past midnight that evening for McCarthy to launch a counteroffensive. Instead, there was silence. His staff said the senator had gone to bed early, had not seen the broadcast, and therefore probably wouldn't bother to reply. This was not like McCarthy, who knew more about the mechanics of what makes news than is taught in the best journalism schools. At any moment during the night he could have topped Murrow's broadcast with an attack on Murrow which, because it would have been later "news," would have received bigger play in the late editions of the morning papers. But for the next twenty-four hours, the news media repeated Murrow's charges without a word from the senator in his own defense. His silence was to prove a grievous miscalculation.

On Thursday morning, March 11, Senator McCarthy entered the Senate Caucus Room a visibly changed man. The bully-boy arrogance was gone. The tic of his head, which usually appeared only under great strain, was now conspicuous. Clearly, his mind was far away from the hearing at which he was supposed to interrogate a frightened black woman named Annie Lee Moss, whom he had accused of being a potential Soviet spy in the Pentagon's top-secret code room.

There was a tortured moment at the start when McCarthy let slip that he didn't even know the name of his prize catch. "Is that Moss or Morse?" he asked counsel Roy Cohn, who quickly supplied the right name. And, after only ten minutes' questioning, the senator suddenly rose from his chair and announced, "I am afraid I am going to have to excuse myself. I've got rather an important appointment tonight which I have got to work on right now." He left with the *See It Now* cameraman Charles Mack filming his exit.

Annie Lee Moss remained in the witness chair, and Cohn tried to pick up the pieces, resorting to the old McCarthy tactic of "secret" information, which Cohn said he possessed proving Moss was or had been a Communist. What followed showed that McCarthy's terrorization of the Senate had at long last come to an end. Dour John McClellan, the segregationist Democratic senator from Arkansas, leaped to the defense of the constitutional liberties of a harassed Negro woman. There was a surge of applause from the audience that doubled when McClellan concluded, "I don't like to try people by hearsay evidence." His arm cut through the air for emphasis. "I like to get the witnesses here and try 'em by testimony under oath." It was a preview of McClellan's formidable opposition during the Army-McCarthy hearings in months to come.

Senator Stuart Symington, the Missouri Democrat, joined in the attack, saying that he might be sticking his neck out, but he thought Mrs. Moss was telling the truth. "If you are not taken back in the Army," he told her, "you come around and see me, and I am going to see that you get a job." A deep sense of charity welled up in the room. And there was wonderful laughter, too—something that hadn't been heard in Washington for a long time—when Symington asked, "Did you ever hear of Karl Marx?" After a moment's bewilderment, a perplexed Annie Lee Moss asked, "Who's that?"

That night, on the Fulton Lewis Jr. radio show, Joe McCarthy finally unleashed his counterattack against Murrow. Out came the hoary exposé of Murrow's connection with the Institute of International Education and the Moscow seminar. Although Murrow had been prepared for this for almost four months, his voice broke with emotion as he went on his own radio broadcast to report McCarthy's accusation. But before the evening was out, the struggle between Edward Roscoe Murrow and Joseph Raymond McCarthy no longer occupied center stage.

For that very night, the Army finally released its full report charging McCarthy and Cohn with trying to finagle special treatment for David Schine. The report would eventually lead to the televised hearings that resulted in the condemnation of McCarthy by the American public and, at long last, the United States Senate. The curtain had opened on the final act of the Rise and Fall of Joe McCarthy, and to Ed Murrow goes a good bit of the credit for raising that curtain.

In a subsequent *See It Now* broadcast, Murrow defended himself against McCarthy's charges, delivering the last, eloquent word on the subject: "It is my devotion to the principles upon which this nation rests—justice, freedom, and fairness—which sets me apart from Senator McCarthy.... When the record is finally written, as it will be one day, it will answer the question: Who has helped the Communist cause and who has served his country better, Senator McCarthy or I? I would like to be remembered by the answer to that question."

# Journalism and McCarthyism
## by Rich Kaplan, Ph.D.

During the early 1950s, Senator Joseph McCarthy, as head of the Senate's Permanent Subcommittee on Investigations of the Senate Committee on Governmental Operations, was able to interrogate, bully, and accuse witnesses of being Communist subversives without letting the victims of his attacks respond. He was also able to take advantage of newspapers, radio, and television to publicize his charges, usually without any serious questioning of his facts. McCarthy's insinuations of Communist subversion were broadcast far and wide. Why did the press become McCarthy's megaphone, publicizing his assertions even when those misrepresentations resulted in harm to innocent victims and a widespread disruption of the American government?

Three factors help account for the press's failure to correct McCarthy: the political climate of the cold war, journalism's own ethic of objectivity, and threats from advertisers and government. One of the most crucial factors was the fear bred by the politics of the cold war. McCarthy's onslaught against Communists seemed like an act of patriotism, and many Americans, politicians, and newspapers lined up behind the anti-Communist senator. Included among the ranks of pro-McCarthy papers were the *Chicago Tribune,* the *New York Daily*

*News,* and the entire chain of papers owned by William Randolph Hearst. Meanwhile, those who doubted the rightness or efficacy of the senator's attacks were branded as unpatriotic, indeed as Communist sympathizers.

As part of their campaign of fear, McCarthy and his allies successfully initiated investigations into the media industries. One after another, journalists or entertainers with either leftist sympathies or past leftist connections were required to sign loyalty oaths or were forced out of the industry. Murrow's network, CBS, in particular, was the repeated target of accusation and scrutiny. Seeking to ward off such attacks, the CBS corporation began screening and firing its employees. Newsman Bob Heller appeared in tears one day at Edward R. Murrow's office. The network had let him go, as well as Robert Shayon. Murrow could do nothing for them, but he tried to defend other veteran reporters, like Alex Kendrick and Howard Smith, from forced termination.

Journalism's normal practices of news reporting, along with the career interests of reporters, also inhibited the press from offering critical assessments of McCarthy. Certainly the press felt compelled to report on the senator. Charges of massive treason and spying issued by a powerful politician were an important news story. Furthermore, McCarthy's story was sensational—it was a good sell, making some reporters' careers. For example, Willard Edwards, a reporter for the *Chicago Tribune,* boasted, "McCarthy was a dream story. I wasn't off of page one for four years."

McCarthy's "facts," however, were crying out for contextualization and assessment, in a word: rebuttal. Here, journalism's ethic of objectivity failed the press and failed the nation. Objectivity does not necessarily mean getting the "truth" as much as making sure one's own interpretation does not intrude into the presentation of information. Part of that information includes what America's political leaders say, no matter whether it is factually right or wrong. Indeed, one might say objectivity hinders any interpretations by a reporter. If the subject were contentious—and communism was certainly that— then the introduction of analysis or assessment by a reporter would be

*Housewife Marie Breetveld holds her son while watching the televised McCarthy-Army hearings on April 22, 1954.*

condemned as subjective, editorializing, or worse—as support for subversives who should not be coddled.

Television broadcasters had their own reasons for not voicing opposition to McCarthyism. Television was a fresh new medium. In 1950, Americans viewed on average only 35 minutes of television a day, while listening to more than four hours of radio, but by the mid-1950s, television had zoomed ahead as the nation's dominant source of information and entertainment. Despite its growing public power, the medium had not yet established its authority to report on public affairs. Television news was a mere 15 minutes a day of headlines, while more serious reporting was reserved for radio and the daily papers. Television thus lacked the authority and prestige to stand up to the might of an angry governmental agency.

The central governmental agency assigned the task of regulating television, as with radio, was the Federal Communications Commission (FCC), which was in charge of station licenses. Only with FCC approval did a broadcaster retain possession of a station license, which was the key to television earnings. In 1953, as he assumed the office of the presidency, Dwight D. Eisenhower appointed two commissioners to the governing board of the FCC. Both were associates of McCarthy, interested in pursuing the senator's agenda of exposing Communists and intimidating those who resisted the witch hunt. In 1954, they demonstrated their willingness to use their newfound powers to take stations from those critical of McCarthy's agenda. Edward Lamb, who owned and operated television stations throughout the South and Midwest, was suddenly notified in the spring of 1954 that his licenses were void. The FCC charged him with having been a member of the Communist party. In truth, Lamb's crime was to have failed to broadcast McCarthy's speeches over his airways. Nonetheless, he was suddenly plunged into a very serious and risky battle for his media holdings.

When Murrow stood up to denounce McCarthy in his March 9, 1954, broadcast of *See It Now,* those pressures were manifest. Those high up in the corporate hierarchy, like CBS chair William Paley, pleaded with Murrow not to wage any political battles with such a fearsome foe. Another consideration against taking on McCarthy was advertising. In the early days of television, each individual show was funded by one corporate sponsor. In effect, the program became an extension of the company's brand name. For Murrow's *See It Now,* Alcoa, the aluminum manufacturer, was the sponsor. That economic funding made each show and each corporate advertiser much more susceptible to any public disapproval stimulated by a broadcast. Public wrath could earmark those corporations that were responsible for support through advertising and make them pay the consequences with boycotts. Already in 1950, anti-Communists had hounded a previous sponsor—Campbell's Soup—into cutting its association with the controversial Murrow. In 1954, supporters of McCarthy began targeting Alcoa. The company was placed under great pressure because of Murrow's words. Nevertheless, Alcoa earned the plaudits of many by refusing to quit its funding.

Despite those pressures, Murrow changed history by challenging McCarthy's demagoguery. Beyond his personal courage and his strong convictions, Murrow possessed unique resources that allowed him to engage in a sustained critical analysis of McCarthy's smear tactics. First and foremost was his reputation, established during World War II. As a CBS radio newscaster stationed in England, he had recounted to Americans back home the daily triumphs and tragedies of America's military forces. He became the country's most trusted newsman in a time of great national worry. In addition, unlike most newscasters, Murrow exercised great power within the broader CBS corporation. He thus could gain the corporation's permission to risk its reputation on a politically dangerous broadcast.

The historical episode of McCarthyism presents important lessons for the responsibilities of the press. The press, far from an independent objective observer of American life, is part and parcel of the American political body. When a climate of patriotic agreement about an enemy reigns at home or abroad, then the press has only limited ability to argue against or rebut the assertions of our government. Many of the resources that sustain our independent press—objectivity, advertising, corporate ownership—risk turning into obstacles that hinder forthright public criticism. Only a press that explicitly recognizes the need for a variety of opinions and strong public debate can avoid the trap of becoming a mere servant of corrupt individuals in government intent on intimidating its opponents into silence.

# "Who'd Know? I'd Know"
## —A Response to Seeing
### *Good Night, and Good Luck*
### *by Howard Weinberg*

"Who'd know? I'd know," said Fred Friendly, often, to those of us teaching with him at Columbia Journalism School in the late 1960s in a special summer program to train minorities in broadcast journalism. How great, I thought, to see dramatized in a feature film the journalistic ethics, social responsibility, and courage that Edward R. Murrow and Fred Friendly shared.

The *See It Now* broadcasts, "The Case of Lieutenant Milo Radulovich," "Annie Lee Moss Before the McCarthy Committee," the famous Murrow compilation of McCarthy clips, McCarthy's reply, and Murrow's answer—all were fresh in my mind as I watched *Good Night, and Good Luck* when it opened the New York Film Festival on September 23, 2005; I had just shown them to my graduate

©2006 Howard Weinberg. Howard Weinberg is an award-winning documentary filmmaker (*Sports for Sale, First Things First, One Plus One, net.LEARNING)* and television journalist (Founding Producer, *The MacNeil/Lehrer Report*; Executive Producer, *Listening to America* with Bill Moyers; Producer, *CBS Sunday Morning* and *Sixty Minutes).* He is an Adjunct Professor in the Graduate Journalism Program at New York University and a Visiting Lecturer in documentary filmmaking at Dartmouth College. He is president of the New York Film/Video Council and a Governor of the New York Chapter of the Television Academy. His website is www.howardweinberg.net.

journalism students at NYU in a CBS program called "The McCarthy Years," narrated by Walter Cronkite.

Shirley Wershba and I had been producers of *The MacNeil/Lehrer Report*. Later, I joined *60 Minutes*, where Joe Wershba was revered as a producer. After seeing the movie, I e-mailed Shirley that she "looked great" on the big screen—to which she replied, "I should have looked as great as Patty Clarkson. It was most flattering."

Very flattering to Fred Friendly as well was George Clooney's matinee idol appearance and relatively subdued portrayal of the executive producer. The Friendly I knew was a larger-than-life creative force, occasionally at odds with his colleagues at Columbia. While teaching and as an adviser to the Ford Foundation, Friendly created a new television form by using Socratic dialogue to force distinguished guests to respond to a hypothetical case history reflecting a major issue in media, law, or public policy. Beginning with a thirteen-part series on *The Constitution: That Delicate Balance*, seventy of these seminars out of the six hundred he commissioned were televised.

Producer Grant Heslov, who co-wrote the film with director George Clooney, played Don Hewitt, the studio director of *See It Now*. Hewitt, whom I worked for after he became the legendary creator of *60 Minutes*, was also an adviser to the film. But it was hard to compare Heslov to Hewitt, for he had a minor role in the film. *Good Night, and Good Luck* emphasized the ensemble, the texture of the times, and kept its focus on Murrow.

Only a month after Murrow's stunning broadcast on CBS on March 9, 1954, ABC-TV carried the Army-McCarthy hearings in full for five weeks. The audience response propelled the fledgling network into real competition with then-dominant CBS and NBC, which carried only excerpts of the hearings. The most memorable moment came when the Army's special counsel Joseph N. Welch said to McCarthy: "Have you no sense of decency sir, at long last? Have you left no sense of decency?" Applause broke out at the hearing, and Welch became an overnight folk hero. Eight months after the Murrow program aired, the Senate could no longer tolerate McCarthy's abuse of his legislative powers, and it censured him by a vote of 65 to 22.

Was it Murrow's *See It Now* broadcast or the televised hearings that followed that led to the demise of Senator Joseph McCarthy? In either case, it was the visual and aural record—McCarthy's own words and behavior captured on film and electronically—that changed public opinion against him. But most of all it was the power of television—and two courageous individuals who served as the conscience of the nation: Murrow and Welch.

Murrow made masterful use of the medium. The effective dramatic storytelling technique of many *See It Now* programs, as in "The Case of Lieutenant Milo Radulovich," focused on a single story that resonated deeply and widely. The other technique used in the McCarthy broadcast and in "Annie Lee Moss Before the McCarthy Committee" was an edited compilation from the public record. When television was new, it had extraordinary power. In later years, it be-

*Edward R. Murrow lights a cigarette for Marilyn Monroe during an interview for the TV series* Person to Person, *April 1, 1955.*

came enamored of the touch-all-bases survey documentary, which dilutes the powerful drama of a single case history, but Murrow's techniques survive in certain documentaries.

Murrow began *Person to Person* in October 1953. How amazing to be able to enter the home of a celebrity, it seemed to most Americans at the time! Though Murrow grew rich from the show and it gained him great popularity, he was said to disdain it. Despite what now seem like awkward live camera switches as the person-of-the-week moved from room to room to show off his home and introduce his spouse, Murrow's talking remotely to a large image on a screen was fascinating and innovative.

Murrow occasionally devoted a program on *See It Now* to a conversation or profile of a prominent figure, such as poet and historian Carl Sandburg, atom bomb scientist J. Robert Oppenheimer, or Prime Minister Nehru of India. Murrow helped television discover its ability to illuminate the human personality. Following closely in his footsteps was Mike Wallace, who captivated me when I was in high school with his well-researched, penetrating late-night TV interviews of guests like Salvador Dali or Governor Orval Faubus of Arkansas, shown in close-up against a black background, often reacting uncomfortably to Wallace's dramatic questions.

\* \* \*

CBS ended *See It Now* in 1955 as a weekly half-hour broadcast after ALCOA dropped its sponsorship. ALCOA had stayed with *See It Now* for a year after the McCarthy broadcast while Murrow kept dealing with controversial issues like nuclear war, civil rights, cigarette smoking and cancer.

*See It Now* appeared occasionally as an hour-long special in 1955. Freed from the weekly broadcast, Murrow increasingly traveled around the world reporting conflict and interviewing controversial political leaders like Marshall Tito of Yugoslavia. CBS followed such interviews with rebuttal panels. For Murrow, who began his career as an educator, reporting political and social controversy conveyed essential information to Americans. For network executives—and for sponsors seeking to polish their image—journalism often could bring

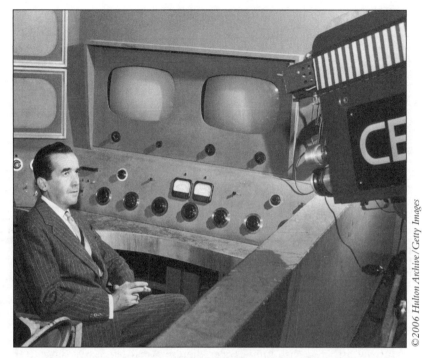

*Promotional portrait of Edward R. Murrow in front of a CBS television camera, January 1955.*

prestige, respect, and honors, but it also carried with it inconvenience and annoyance. When controversial reporting threatened profits and business relationships, it became anathema.

After *See It Now* ended in 1958, Murrow started the less well-known, innovative *Small World*, a filmed series of international telephone conversations with three important political or cultural figures. Sometimes the program mixed outstanding minds from different walks of life. *Small World*'s debut featured Aldous Huxley in Turin, Italy; Pandit Nehru in New Delhi, India; and Thomas E. Dewey in Portland, Maine. The interviewees were filmed simultaneously and the film flown to New York and edited for broadcast. For Murrow, it was a consolation prize after the cancellation of *See It Now*. *Small World* debuted in October 1958, a few days before Murrow's famous "wires in a box" speech to the Radio-Television News Director's Association that opens and closes *Good Night, and Good Luck.*

\* \* \*

McCarthyism lived on in the broadcast industry until the early 1960s, but Senator McCarthy himself, his liver ruined by alcohol, died of acute hepatitis at the age of forty-nine in May 1957. Murrow continued his role as conscience of the nation in 1960 as correspondent for a new *CBS Reports* documentary on the plight of migrant workers, *Harvest of Shame*. That and the McCarthy broadcasts are the twin pillars of his legacy. Finding life increasingly difficult at CBS, Murrow surprised colleagues by accepting President John F. Kennedy's offer to head the United States Information Agency. In that capacity, Murrow tried to censor programs the television networks sold to foreign countries. Amazingly, he asked the BBC not to broadcast *Harvest of Shame*, but his request was refused. At USIA Murrow hired some who had suffered during the McCarthy era. Murrow, afflicted with lung cancer, died in April 1965, two days after his fifty-seventh birthday.

Fred Friendly went on to produce a series of innovative *CBS Reports* documentaries such as "The National Driver's Test"; but in 1966, when CBS refused to broadcast live the Senate Foreign Relations Committee's hearings on Vietnam, Friendly resigned.

Television had changed. CBS was making money with shows like *The Beverly Hillbillies*. Opportunities for serious journalism were few. It wasn't until the Watergate scandal and, nearly twenty years later, the confirmation hearings of Clarence Thomas's appointment to the Supreme Court that televised hearings would again play a role in galvanizing a mass audience. Today, even with twenty-four-hour cable news channels yearning for a running story, the multitude of channels are controlled by a few conglomerates focused on the bottom line, and the potential audience is fractured. It's hard to imagine that public hearings ever again will be able to rivet an audience or bring a politician public acclaim or disgrace. Or that a courageous television journalist could hope to make an impact on American society as did Edward R. Murrow. But seeing *Good Night, and Good Luck* and hearing Murrow's final words might just inspire someone in a new generation to try: "*There is a great and perhaps decisive battle to be fought against ignorance, intolerance and indifference. This weapon of television could be useful. Stonewall Jackson, who knew something about the use of weapons, is reported to have said, 'When war comes, you must draw the sword and throw away the scabbard.' The trouble with television is that it is rusting in the scabbard during a battle for survival.*"

# Part Two:
# The Movie

STILLS

David Strathairn as Edward R. Murrow

Matt Ross as Eddie Scott, David Strathairn as Edward R. Murrow, Tate Donovan as Jesse Zousmer, and Reed Diamond as John Aaron

David Strathairn as Edward R. Murrow

David Strathairn as Edward R. Murrow and George Clooney as Fred Friendly

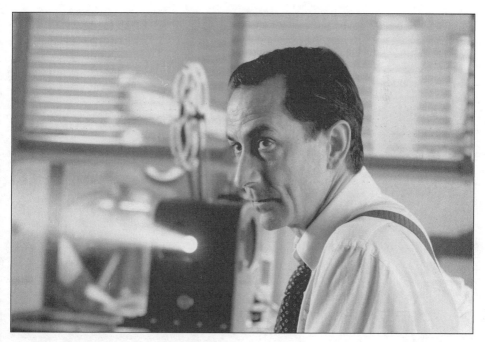

David Strathairn as Edward R. Murrow

George Clooney as Fred Friendly and David Strathairn as Edward R. Murrow

Robert Downey Jr. as Joe Wershba

Jeff Daniels as Sig Mickelson

Patricia Clarkson as Shirley Wershba and Robert Downey Jr. as Joe Wershba

George Clooney as Fred Friendly

David Strathairn as Edward R. Murrow

Ray Wise as Don Hollenbeck

George Clooney as Fred Friendly and David Strathairn as Edward R. Murrow

David Strathairn as Edward R. Murrow

Tate Donovan as Jesse Zousmer and Grant Heslov as Don Hewitt

Director George Clooney on the set of *Good Night, and Good Luck* with Frank Langella and David Strathairn

George Clooney as Fred Friendly, Glenn Morshower as Colonel Anderson, and Don Creech as Colonel Jenkins

Patricia Clarkson as Shirley Wershba

Frank Langella as William Paley

Three-time Grammy® Award–winning jazz singer Dianne Reeves

Tom McCarthy as Palmer Williams (foreground) and David Strathairn as Edward
R. Murrow (background)

Tate Donovan as Jesse Zousmer

Director George Clooney on the set of *Good Night, and Good Luck* with Ray Wise
and producer/co-writer Grant Heslov

David Strathairn as Edward R. Murrow

Grant Heslov as Don Hewitt

Robert Downey Jr. as Joe Wershba, Patricia Clarkson as Shirley Wershba, George Clooney as Fred Friendly, David Strathairn as Edward R. Murrow, and Tate Donovan as Jesse Zousmer

George Clooney as Fred Friendly

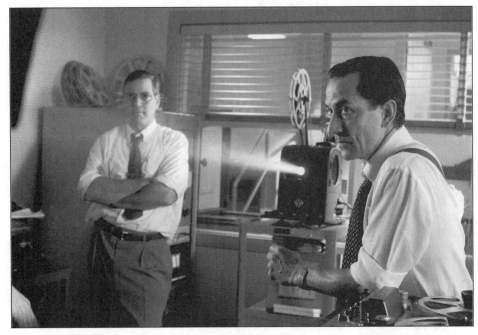

George Clooney as Fred Friendly and David Strathairn as Edward R. Murrow

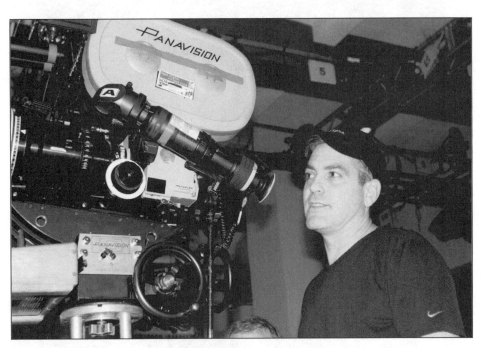

Director George Clooney on the set

# About the Production

For George Clooney, the co-writer and director of *Good Night, and Good Luck*, it was his fascination with the famed broadcast journalist Edward R. Murrow, played by David Strathairn, that proved to be the inspiration for his telling of one of the most important political upheavals in American history. His father had been a news anchor for thirty years and Murrow was a hero to his family, a man every news journalist aspired to be.

For years, Clooney had thoughts of filming something about him. He wrote a TV movie and even considered making a live TV movie in the tradition of his live airing of *Fail-Safe*. For multiple reasons, neither was produced. Clooney was conscious that he didn't want to make a straightforward biopic. This was an opportunity, among other things, to explore the nature and power of television through one of its most revered personalities. Eventually, he and producer and co-writer Grant Heslov (who plays the role of Don Hewitt) decided that Murrow would best be depicted in a feature film set during a specific time period. Specifically, they focused on the early 1950s, during Senator McCarthy's Communist witch hunts and the televised conflicts between the two. Says Clooney, "This incident and time has been a passion of mine because it is one of the few times you could point to where broadcast journalism actually changed the world and people's minds. McCarthy was untouchable until Murrow stepped up. It was one of those great moments where you really had to be brave."

David Strathairn is the exceptional actor who plays Murrow, and he also sees the film as an opportunity both to examine the man and to learn about a specific time in American history: "Edward R. Murrow was a true American hero, a legend in his own time, although there are not as many people around who really remember him. So, from that point of view, it's really informative. The facts are in there and the history is in there, too. It's compelling."

The filmmakers felt that the on-air conflict between Murrow and McCarthy is, at its heart, a great story. It shows two titans at the peak of their powers as they confront each other, and end both of their careers by doing so. It was important to make the point that Murrow is remembered by most as a great American, while McCarthy is remembered as someone who used fear to gain popularity. Murrow's (and his team's) sense of moral justice and general human decency make him a hero of the highest order.

Clooney's deep connection can be felt by the other actors. Strathairn maintains that there is nothing Clooney doesn't know about the subject, and makes a good analogy: "He's really the Edward R. Murrow of this production and Grant is the Fred Friendly. These guys have put together a world and a group of people and an amazing crew where everybody's on the same page. You feel like there's this momentum of energy and that we're making something special."

Both Clooney and Heslov wanted to create an accurate portrayal of the time, so verisimilitude was the key. A conscious effort was made to incorporate many of the speeches made by the people at the time, including McCarthy and Murrow. Although many of the real-life people played in the film are portrayed by actors, they decided to divert from the norm and portray McCarthy through the use of real footage. Heslov says, "We realized that whomever we got to play McCarthy, no matter how good they were, nobody was going to believe it.... In regard to Murrow's speeches, here was all this great writing, so why not use it? We just felt very strongly that his speeches were so beautiful." If they could come close to delivering some of Murrow's ideas as cleanly as possible, they would accomplish what they were after.

Strathairn remembers how the initial script read-through was quite daunting because of the presence of many of the real-life characters. It was at this point that he began to feel the importance of accuracy: "Milo Radulovich was there, Fred Friendly's two sons and one of his wives was there, there was the real Joe and Shirley Wershba. Everybody had come in for the table read, which is almost unheard-of in film production." He continues: "To listen to them speak and see all the photographs, to look at the documentation of *See It Now,* is a huge challenge to access but deserves the attempt."

Of course, playing such a towering, important figure as Murrow would be a daunting task for any actor. Clooney even considered himself for the role at one stage. Yet, according to Heslov, he and Clooney knew it was no contest once they had met Strathairn: "We knew he was a great actor but you still can't tell, particularly when it's playing somebody as iconic as Murrow. However, the second he was in front of the camera, and started doing some of those huge speeches, he was transformed. I've been with a lot of actors and I'd never seen anybody as transformed to the point where I'd look up and forget that it wasn't Murrow. It was uncanny, but he's brilliant."

Clooney concurs, as an established actor himself, that it was vital to get the right look. Also, he didn't want just an impersonator, but someone who captures the essence of the character: "We got on the set and started rehearsing and it seemed fine. David had long hair and a beard, but then he shaved and he slicked his hair back and started talking. We all just sat there with our mouths open."

While shooting in black and white was a choice they made, it also proved, in terms of production design, a lot more forgiving than color. Clooney says, "We had to film Joe Wershba, played by Robert Downey Jr., and then play that back on a TV screen and then film that. We basically took the Joe Wershba from the 1950s and replaced him with the Robert Downey Jr. of 2005 and then intercut that with the old footage back and forth." For his part, Downey Jr. got to meet the real thing. "He's just a great guy. He really only had one note for me and just said, 'We were really aggressive. Don't forget that, kid, we really loved what we were doing.'"

During the shoot, the *See It Now* set was authentically replicated and designed so the camera could move freely in any direction. It was almost like going back in time to the CBS studios of the 1950s. Detail was paramount. The props department even delivered newspapers from the early '50s with their headlines corresponding to the script day. According to Production Designer Jim Bissell, Clooney wanted a way to create a space that would incorporate three different locations, in order to follow the actors around from one place to another. "The other mandate was to try to create depth to the sets with very little money, make it feel big without really spending anything because we had strict budget limitations. One way was by incorporating the glass end so you could see through and you would have the depth and be able to rack focus to see different activities going on at the same time."

The focus on the reality of the events as they played out is exemplified through the use of actual footage and documented speeches. For Clooney, the focal point wasn't on the characters' personal lives because it wasn't relevant: "This is specifically about a television event. And I wanted only the moments that played out on television. We stayed away from most of the exploitative facts, and we just tried to stick with basics."

The writers also wanted to capture that frenetic, live energy feeling the show used to have when it was broadcast. They decided to foster improvised situations on set. After making the improvised HBO series *Unscripted,* says Clooney, "Grant and I really fell in love with multiple cameras and people talking on top of each other and all the things that I liked from the films of the '70s. It's a very tricky thing, though, because we're playing in 1953 and 1954, and it's a very different aesthetic and we had to find that happy medium of feeling. People don't improvise the way they talked in 1953, so we'd give actors newspapers and everything they could possibly need to get prepared to shoot for thirty minutes for a minute-and-a-half scene. That, to me, was the exciting part."

Yet, Clooney was very specific about boundaries too. A lot of people in the movie were on hand during the shoot to act as a witness and a reference. "We asked Joe and Shirley Wershba every day, 'Where are we wrong? What are we missing in this?' That was what was important to us because we had to treat these questions in many ways the same way that Murrow treated things, which was that we had to double-source our material."

The film has an impressive array of top-quality actors that includes Patricia Clarkson, Jeff Daniels, Tate Donovan, Frank Langella, and Ray Wise. They all relished the idea of joining an ensemble piece. Actor Jeff Daniels, who plays Sig Mickelson, says, "After forty films, you want to do stuff that matters, and this is a good project with good people. It's timely and I liked being part of that." Actress Patricia Clarkson, who plays Shirley Wershba, the only main female character, quickly began to trust and feel confident in her director: "He's always right on. The improv is always exactly the idea of the concept. And he only says something when he has to, and his direction is incredibly eloquent and succinct."

Downey Jr. says it's been rewarding to watch Clooney and Heslov work as a team, "At the end of the day you can't really care too much or you're going to blow it. They're very close to the material but also have a healthy dose of detachment and levity, considering the subject matter is not light."

Clooney found this experience of directing much different from his debut effort, *Confessions of a Dangerous Mind.* His first movie had the luxury of shooting time that was three times longer. This was a quick shoot that took six weeks and was shot on a low budget. Also, having undergone back and neck surgery at Christmas, he almost pulled the plug.

Daniels says, "Everything's so cyclical. Everything comes back and history sometimes does repeat itself if we allow it. I think it's good to remind everyone on both sides of the aisle that we've been through this already and we should learn from that. America wants to be nothing but safe; we also want our art and our culture to be safe. We want everything to be safe. This story speaks volumes to me."

Finally, Clooney has this to say, "There's an opportunity that one in a hundred young kids actually might learn who Murrow is and have some discussion and have some understanding of what and how dangerous a democracy can be if fear is used as a weapon."

# Q & A with
# George Clooney and Grant Heslov

The following interview was conducted over a few days in November 2005 in Los Angeles, California, by Rob Feld.

*Tell me how the project originated with you and about your process of collaboration. Were you in the room together or working individually?*

**GEORGE CLOONEY:** It started with a project that I had been working on or interested in for a while. I called Grant up and said I think we can make a movie out of this.

**GRANT HESLOV:** George's father is a broadcast journalist, so George grew up in the world of local news. Murrow was somebody who was held in high regard in his home, and I've known George for a long time. We've been friends for over twenty years and I know his folks. I knew a little about Murrow, but I learned a lot more through my friendship with George and his parents. And then, I guess it was about six or seven years ago, George wanted to write a TV movie about Murrow, which he did. It was more biopic. It was told through the eyes of a fictional character and was a very different kind of story.... Ultimately it didn't get made; he just sort of put it in a drawer. And then about three and a half years ago we started talking about Murrow again, thinking, Wouldn't it be cool to do a feature, inter-linking all that we learned in the years since? We'd done a series together, and George and I have both acted in or worked on lots of films during that time. So we decided to give it a crack.

**GC:** I outlined it based on some television shows that I had grown up with and was sort of aware of, and in the process started hacking through the outline, stuff that we needed to research. Grant went in and started doing the heavy-duty researching, because he's really good at that. We had a partners' desk that we sat at, and would go back and forth. Basically, from the minute we started, we decided to start out as if we were journalists, because we figured in this day and age anything you get inaccurate, you get beat up. So we started double-sourcing everything.

**GH:** We did about a year and a half of research, and we went to New York, and we met with Joe and Shirley Wershba and Don Hewitt. We met with Milo Radulovich and we talked to Fred Friendly's family and Casey, Murrow's son. We tried to talk to everyone who was still alive that we could get our hands on. We read every book that we could find and watched every documentary, watched the *See It Now* and *Person to Person* shows. It took a while.

**GC:** I'd already set an outline of what the story was, so the next step was to try and go out and get as much information as we could, including the arguments against our point of view, which I thought was important. So we went through all the Columbia Journalism School arguments about editorializing for the first time, for and against what Murrow did. Then we were able to raise an argument, rather than make it just a one-sided affair.

**GH:** Once we did that, we started to figure out and noodle with the scope of the story that we wanted to tell. We knew that we didn't want to do a traditional biopic.

*How did you decide on this particular slice of time, shying away from a traditional biopic format—that survey of a person's life—which can be a hazardous thing?*

**GH:** We were more interested in a seminal moment in history, George often talked about the moment when Walter Cronkite went to Vietnam and came back and said, "This is not a winnable war." It changed the psyche of America and was really a turning point in what the country did vis-à-vis the Vietnam War. This was a similar seminal moment, from beginning to end.

**GC:** From the very beginning when I sat down with Grant, I said, "This is a story about five episodes of TV." That was what was important to me. There's some people whose lives are really interesting and great, and Murrow's is certainly an amazing, interesting story. But rather than telling the story of him doing the London blitz and then dying of lung cancer at the end, we thought it was more important to take the highest point, the greatest moment of the guy who was considered the beacon of broadcast journalism's life, and focus on that rather than dilute it with other story lines. Those are the kind of biopics I'm interested in, which are not biopics at all. They're sort of specific moments in time.

*Is that an easier or better film to make, from a storytelling point of view?*
**GC:** Actually, in a way, I think it's more difficult because we're not doing the fun parts, which are at home with the wife, or whatever. There can be a lot of easy, natural drama if you take it home and hear what people's thoughts and fears are. That's a lot easier than trying to convey it with silence in a newsroom, between a bunch of people. For us the challenge was to try and keep it alive and moving inside the walls of the one place where it really mattered—which was that room. It was about trying to create and remind people of the paranoia that existed, without having someone say it—if you go home with them, they say it—and we thought the job was not to have them say it as much as to have them feel and experience it.

*Tell me about the idea of "a little picture."*
**GH:** That was something Murrow talked a lot about, and actually much in the way that Murrow uses Radulovich as a little picture, we used this episode of history as a little picture, even though it's a big idea and was a big moment in our history. We wanted to use this as Arthur Miller used the Salem witch hunts in *The Crucible*. Now, if we're a tenth as successful as he was, then I'll be happy.

*Basically, it's metaphor, then: an accessible way to enter and communicate a story or greater idea. The essence of storytelling.*
**GC:** Right. It is. You have to remember that Murrow was never a

news anchor. He did what *60 Minutes* became—a magazine show that deals with news subjects—but he wasn't doing regular news. So the idea was that they were still trying to tell stories. It wasn't just, "Hey, here's the news." His job was to try and tell a story. And they were very good at doing that in "Harvest of Shame," with the migrant farmworkers. With the important shows that he did over the years, he did them very specifically about a specific group of people, rather than trying to talk about a big general subject that would lose punch.

**GH:** Initially, thematically, we wanted to explore the idea that real news is getting pushed out more and more, and ask that question, "Is it?" As we were writing, and started to put it all together, we started to see that a lot of the things our characters were talking about were no different than they are now, and that a lot of the things they were talking about seemed to be repeating themselves to varying degrees. I certainly don't think that the times are as dire as they were. People's civil liberties aren't being trampled on to the extent that they were then, but there are a lot of things happening, and we thought that this story spoke to a lot of those issues.

*So the "little picture," the micro view, was the safe way to present the McCarthy story to people?*

**GC:** Murrow didn't want to go directly at McCarthy, because he thought that that would just look like a giant swing by a network at a senator. And, quite honestly, they were trying to avoid it. Remember that TV was one of the last in. Newspapers had already gone after McCarthy a little bit. Murrow wasn't the first journalist to go at him—he was just by far the most popular and famous. He was playing with a bigger audience and was the most trusted man in America. His rationale was, I can do this if I make it only about a little picture, somebody's personal story. You know, I'll tell you the best version of that is with that *Extreme Home Makeover* show. If they were just saying, "Let's go fix up people's homes" or "Let's fix a village," it would be sort of like those telethons you see, where everybody's going, "Let's go help the poor." Instead, what they do is they take one person's life, tell you about it, and then make you care about that one person, while they try to help them. So Murrow felt that Radulovich was a way in.

Ann Coulter just came out with a thing the other day, where she gets all her facts wrong. The one that I love is where she claims that Radulovich had nothing to do with McCarthy. Certainly, Radulovich did have to do with the policies that McCarthy was setting, like the idea that you weren't allowed to face your accuser. What the people who criticize the analysis get wrong is that Radulovich had nothing to do with McCarthy directly until Don Surine, who worked for Hoover and under McCarthy, grabbed Joe Wershba, handed him an envelope, and said that since he'd done the Radulovich story, they were going to prove that Murrow was a spy. And that actually was directly to do with McCarthy. So, the truth is, it was McCarthy's mistake. He made the mistake of getting overconfident, because no one was really coming at him. And he went at Murrow at the exact wrong time. He lost the argument, ultimately, not because Murrow went at McCarthy, but because McCarthy, in his rebuttal, turned around and accused Murrow of being a traitor. And everyone knew that wasn't true. That, to me, was the beauty of this story: it's never the attack. It's drawing somebody in and letting them destroy themselves.

*The classic fatal flaw. Tell me about how you used silence for effect. Reading the script, it actually seems very skeletal, but you created deep atmosphere in the film.*

**GH:** In this case, silence was there to build tension. Those silent moments before a broadcast, where it's just Friendly tapping Murrow's foot. It's that kind of silence, and allowing that silence to be. Even when we went in to mix, the sound guys wanted to mix in all kinds of noises and stuff, but George just said, *"No.* We want it to be this. We don't want it to feel Foley'ed." And throughout the piece, there are a lot of moments of those silences.

**GC:** When we first sat down with the studio, they said, "Too few pages." Probably my favorite film of all time is *Fail-Safe.* It had no musical score and used silence to build tension. Silence was actually the score in the movie. I used that as a reference point from the very beginning. You know, as the MTV generation—and I think I was the first of it; it came out when I was twenty—we've gotten to that point where people think that if you don't have fifteen different things going on at the same time, like Bloomberg television, you can't hold an audience's attention. But I find that if I'm flipping the channels and I find pure silence on, that's the thing that stops me now. So I thought it was an interesting thing to talk about and use as the score, rather than steering away from it.

**GH:** The silences are a great juxtaposition to the bigger, loud, exciting scenes, like the end of a show where everybody's up and clapping. Also, then, to give a chance for the audience to decompress. Some of those silences we filled with some Dianne Reeves stuff. In a way, we came to see her as our Greek chorus.

*That's an interesting notion, using Reeves as the chorus, giving some counterpoint, especially considering you so rarely leave the studio and engage other characters, so you have little other opportunity for that.*

**GH:** The songs are thematically connected to either the scene they appear in or the piece as a whole, but they're also transition moments, almost all of them. For instance, I think one of the most effective uses of Dianne is at the end of the first Radulovich show. Friendly says, "And we're out," and everybody in the place goes crazy. But instead of hearing that, we go to Dianne and hear her singing a song, because as George was cutting the thing, he realized we can't just keep going to the guys celebrating every time. It has to be different, otherwise it's going to be redundant. So, it was great for that. "How High the Moon," to us, was just a beautiful counterpoint to hearing the article read; hearing her and seeing her sing, and then just seeing the effect on Murrow and the guys. What was also interesting about that part of the film was that it was all done live—whenever you see her singing, that's her. It's not lip-synched. It was all played live because there's nothing worse than when you can tell somebody's not really singing. But beyond that, there's a sound quality. There's an energy that you just can't get any other way.

In the first scene of the film, after the bookend—the speech—there's two women getting in an elevator. They come out and we follow them. We hear the singing—we hear it over the speaker, then we hear it fill the room, and we hear it as they come in and one of them says something to Tate, and walks over to the door, and opens up the stage door to look in. She's singing that live the whole time. We had to time it out so that when the door opened, it was on the piece of the song that we wanted to emphasize at that moment. We decided, let's pick four, five, or six songs that somehow speak to the film, without hitting anything over the head. So we did and just said, "Rehearse those." We shot them all, and some of them we used. Some of them we just used under stuff. But having those moments with Dianne lets the audience take a breath, because a lot comes at them. We don't explain a lot right out of the gate. I know that the audience is not sure who these characters are. They know that they're all part of some group that's doing something, but it takes a while to catch up. We were very aware of that. We always wanted people to be behind us, never ahead. So those moments were built specifically to put more air in there and take some time, and then move into the next piece.

*How did you deal with that issue of exposition and keeping ahead of the audience? What did you feel people had to know, and did you find it was less than you thought?*

**GH:** As you see in the film, we have almost no exposition; we wanted to plop the audience right in the middle of the action. Some older audience members have very vivid memories of the period, but many don't, and we didn't want the film to be a history lesson. Even if you know nothing about that period, I still think you can follow the film and see its parallels to the present.

*How did you approach creating Murrow and, perhaps, the difference between impersonation and interpretation? What are the pitfalls of portraying an icon?*

**GC:** Well, remember that I did *Confessions of a Dangerous Mind*, which was about a famous guy, and Sam Rockwell was wonderful in it. The trick in that one was, I wanted somebody who could play Chuck Barris without an impersonation, because the simple truth is that not many people were going to remember Barris. A few people will recognize some of the things he did, but the most important thing was that he had to carry a film. So you can't just rest things on a Rich Little impression. You have to rest it on a real character study.

**GH:** We wanted to underwrite him, in a way. Obviously, the character carries the film on his back. David does a brilliant job with those speeches. They're beautiful speeches, and we wanted that character to feel like when he spoke, it mattered. So we didn't want him to get as involved in the scenes with all the guys pitching ideas. We wanted him to sit back in those moments and let the scenes happen around him.

**GC:** The first thing to do is cast the right guy. That's all you have to do as a director. I was tempted to play the part myself, for a minute. Until you really realize that the secret and the essence of Murrow is that you always felt as if Edward R. Murrow was carrying the weight of all of our sins on his shoulders. There's always this sadness to him, which is not a quality that people inherently attribute to me. You can't act that, you can only cast that. And David Strathairn, in every movie he's ever played, has this gravitas and this weight and this sadness to him. He looks enough like him. In fact, he looks tremendously like him, once he did the movie. He's a great actor and I knew he was the right guy to do the part. His voice was a little higher than Murrow's, but I primarily needed a really good actor, not to do an impersonation, because not enough people are ever going to remember Murrow, anyway—it just so happens he does an impeccable impersonation. But first and foremost, we needed an actor who could carry scenes and carry the way people talked in the 1950s, which is a very different way than now. It's much cleaner and simpler and less descriptive. And he is the perfect actor for it.

*Yes, how did you approach that? It was a much more formal time.*

**GH:** Well, one thing was that people weren't sloppy with their speech. George talked to the guys about that a lot. And then you put on those clothes, you get your hair greased back, and you sort of fall into that period. A lot of smoke, a lot of smoking. One of the great things was that a bunch of those guys were friends of ours, like Tate Donovan, Reed Diamond, and Tommy McCarthy. They're all guys that we knew, and Reed and Tate had worked with David before in another film, *Memphis Belle*. So there was a lot of camaraderie, which is just testament to George's casting. Half the battle is to try to get people to believe the people on-screen have a history.

**GC:** People related in a very different way. They never talked about what they were really feeling. They spoke very clearly and succinctly, and didn't say much. There was a chivalry between the guys and girls. There was a different way of addressing each other. There were also certainly things like sending Patty outside to get the newspapers, because she's the girl. There was a sort of a World War II stoicism, like "Yeah, we know we're scared," but nobody says, "I'm scared." You just go, "All right, let's go get them." And there's something really attractive about that. At least it is to me.

*In the script there was a bit that didn't make it into the film: the way we meet Murrow. It's right after the bookend speech scene, as the writers are pitching ideas. Murrow is silent and somebody asks him, "What rhymes with bucket?" and he says, "Pail." Even though it didn't make it in, what did that bit say about the character that made you initially choose it as an introduction?*

**GH:** I have to credit George with that line. I just think that Murrow was a guy who had a sense of humor. In the first shot you get of him in that scene, it's very quiet. They're watching footage of McCarthy and there's a fairly intense shot of Murrow. I think we wanted to show the camaraderie and the sort of working relationship that these guys all had, but also the hierarchy. Nobody called him Ed except for Fred, which was true. Everyone called him Mr. Murrow. There was a pecking order and we wanted to establish that.

**GC:** It didn't stick to script in those scenes. Those scenes inside that room were basically improvised. We would give each of the kids, like, three newspapers from that day, say, October 4th, 1954. They'd come in a couple of hours early, sit down, go through the papers for two hours, pick their stories, and type them on the manual typewriter. Then they'd come into the room and I'd sit there like my dad used to do as the news director and go, "Okay, what's your story? What's your lead?" And have them each pick their story. So it was also an improvisation. That was the first week of shooting, and I realized that the secret to making someone powerful in a room, especially a room like this, with so many characters, was silence, again. The less Murrow spoke, the more powerful he was, the more we deferred to him. You

know, he's only as powerful as the other characters in the film make
him. So, he doesn't have to talk much, but when he does, like on the
air, it actually speaks volumes.

*I thought that one of the successes of the film was creating that collegial-
ity and the repartee of the newsroom.*
**GC:**  Well, that was also part of the plan. You know, I'd grown up on
the floor of newsrooms, watching how news was made with my dad.
And these guys were all sort of hard-nosed guys; they drank and they
smoked and they made jokes and it was gallows humor, and they just
kept going. The one thing you always felt was that no matter what
their personalities were, they had a certain line that they agreed was
what was important. And that line was breaking a story, getting the
news and fighting for it through everything, through corporate inter-
ference, everything. The most important thing you could do was get
information and break it. There was great competition between them,
but there was also great camaraderie. These actors, most of the guys
knew each other, and that was part of it. We didn't read any actors for
their roles. We just knew these guys.
**GH:**  Another thing is that all those scenes are written in dual dialogue, so everything was meant to overlap. We wanted it to feel like it
really does when a group of people are working together. Generally,
everyone is talking over each other, not always listening. Often, the
way you see it in a film, a period film in particular, it's one person
speaking, everybody's listening, and then another person reacts.

*The studio space was also something of a character in and of itself. You
spend almost all of your time in there. Were you concerned that was
going to be difficult or constraining, being so hermetically sealed?*
**GC:**  Well, the financial constraints make a difference. You're not actually able to leave the studio because, quite honestly, we couldn't
afford it. But sometimes those kinds of problems end up helping you.
What we were trying to do was create a claustrophobic world, and the
more we went outside it, the less easy it would have been to make the
outside world seem scary. So staying inside that room and talking
about how scary it is out there, you can keep it pretty scary. To us it
was a bunker and you could get inside the bunker, like Henry Fonda

and Larry Hagman do in *Fail-Safe*. Keep inside the bunker and talk about how dangerous things are, and it usually works.

**GH:** Jim Bissell designed the studio, and George told him what his needs were; he wanted to be able to shoot in any direction at any time. He wanted to be able to look through glass and see other rooms. He wanted to be able to see people working in the background when scenes were going on in the foreground. He wanted to be able to build a stage so that one minute it's *See It Now*, where they did the news, and then could convert, like the way it was where he grew up.

**GC:** I grew up at a television station that was a newsroom, but they also did variety shows in the same soundstage, with a bowling alley underneath the news thing. They'd pick up the news desks at the end of the news, peel it away, there's a bowling alley underneath it for *Bowling for Dollars* at 7:30. Then they'd shoot a variety show on top of that, and a band would come in and play. Then they'd pull that out and put the news desks back in for the 11:00 news. I loved the idea of not just telling the story, but physically watching entertainment and news having to sort of push each other off the set, all the time. And I thought that that was a good thing to be able to do with Dianne.

**GH:** That was how the Dianne Reeves thing worked in: things just got pushed aside, and then another set came in. The truth about the real-life studio was that there were three of them in New York. There were the corporate offices, there were their offices where they did all the writing, and then there was the actual studio. But for the purposes of our film, we combined it all. We wanted it to feel like it was an office building, so George had Jim Bissell design this sort of rotating elevator. The actors could get in the elevator, it would rotate, and the doors would open in a different part of the set. George wanted to do that in the very beginning, because he felt like once we put people in an elevator, you'd feel like you were in a building and people wouldn't question it again. Another interesting thing about the set is that, because we were shooting in black and white, the whole thing was painted in monochromatic colors. Basically what Jim did is, we did a test. They painted these boards ten or fifteen different colors and put numbers on them. Then, as we were doing camera tests one day, we shot them, and he decided what color he would paint everything.

Then he would just walk around the set and write the number on the walls, and the guys would come by and paint the piece that number, which was kind of cool. It didn't look far from what you really would imagine it to look like, because the truth is, you'd imagine that period in black and white anyway. So it was pretty close. We also wanted it to be so that we could be pre-lit on everything, so there wasn't a lot of setup time for lighting. We didn't want to have a lot of waiting around time.

*Did you have concerns about never leaving this space?*
**GH:** We didn't have concerns because it was by design. We wanted it to feel claustrophobic. We wanted it to feel oppressive in the way that we felt it must have felt back then. We were also strapped by budgetary constraints, and once you get outside and try to recreate a period, it gets tough. There is one exterior shot, with the folks looking at the TV, but barely. We never go wide enough that you would know. We did shoot a few. We shot one on the fly. One day, George said, "You know what? Let's throw some of the guys in a car and just shoot them." We thought maybe if we shot with long lenses—so the background would be out of focus—and went downtown and shot at night, it would look like Manhattan. It just didn't work. It just didn't fit into the film. So we weren't concerned, but it was definitely a conscious choice.

*What did you find to be your greatest hurdle in making this story work and be compelling? Were you concerned that it would become a didactic history lesson?*
**GH:** Well that was *the* hurdle. Well, it really wasn't *our* hurdle, because we knew it would be fine. It was other people's hurdles. I guess the biggest hurdle once we wrote it was to convince people that a lot of what was going to happen wasn't on the page. A lot of what was going to happen was in the silence, and you can't write silence. George was very specific about how he wanted to use silence, and had a very strong vision of how he wanted things to look, sound, and feel, which we were able to incorporate into the screenplay, and which I was able to understand at a very early stage because we wrote it together. Initially, we had no music in the piece at all. Actually that's not

true. We always had "How High the Moon," when Hollenbeck kills himself. Before we even started writing the piece, we knew we were going to have Hollenbeck's suicide in it, and that somebody was going to be singing that song. It was only after we hired Dianne and started filming that we added more songs to it. It was a hurdle to help people understand what that was going to be like, what these silences were going to be like.

**GC:** Well, I wasn't worried about it being a didactic history lesson, because we'd done *Unscripted.* I've been working on films and producing and writing projects for a long time, and I knew how to make it entertaining. I wasn't really worried about that. Our biggest hurdle was making sure that there was a blend between McCarthy—the actual footage—and our real guys, the actors. The trick was not only to make sure that the acting style was the same style that they spoke in back then, so it didn't stand out, but it also meant that, in general, whenever you saw footage of the original stuff, we had to put it in a place that was not artificial. We weren't trying to *Forrest Gump* it, where you try to match film stocks and you think it's actually somebody standing in a room talking. By placing it on a television or projection screen, that footage could always have a difference and yet still feel like it's part of the actual story, as opposed to taking you out of it. Usually you'll find that original footage in a movie, from some other event, immediately makes you go, "Ugh." So, if you could put it in a different medium, project it on a screen, on a television monitor, you were able to get just enough separation, instead of trying to directly match something and then make sure that the acting styles were similar.

*Did that also play into your decision to shoot in black and white?*
**GC:** From the very beginning, yeah. Although, I must say, also, from the very beginning, I knew I was going to do it in black and white, because I've never seen Edward R. Murrow or Joe McCarthy in color. Ever. I don't know them in color, and I thought that was an important part of it. And this is a black and white story, you know? Believe me, nobody was thrilled. It made it almost impossible to get the budget for the film. But that's okay, we got it.

*It must have been hard for people to visualize. The script is very skeletal.*
**GH:** Looking back at it, I can now understand what some people thought and might not have understood. The original script we had was eighty-five pages, and I actually had to add five pages just to get the bond company to agree. Then we ended up adding a couple more scenes and it got a little bit longer, but we knew that we always wanted a movie that was ninety minutes. To get people to sit still for a couple of hours on material that's not car chases and action, there's really no need to go any longer, for us, anyway. Back to your last question, the real trick was figuring the puzzle of how much to use of each piece of footage. How much Annie Lee Moss do we want to use? What do we want to use? Because there's a lot of footage from all these things. Which pieces of McCarthy? Even though we didn't write McCarthy's dialogue, we had to pre-pick it, edit it, and figure out what it was all going to say and mean. So that was among the most challenging things.

*You chose something of a documentary aesthetic. How did that play into the narrative? There's a tension that creates.*
**GC:** We started with the sort of the Godard theory and we thought about shooting on Super 16 with those lenses, the ones he used—sort of gaffers taping them to the camera—and then realizing that that was actually, in a way, too artistic a way to shoot this. We watched Pennebaker documentaries and Drew documentaries like *Primary* and *Crisis*. We started focusing on the idea that we had to shoot it as if we were in the room. In *Confessions of a Dangerous Mind*, I made the camera a character in the movie. Literally, it was one of the characters in the movie. You were always aware of the camera, physically, because it was sort of a fantasy story. This one, since it's based on reality, I felt like I needed to focus more on documentary-style footage, and that we really had to run two cameras. We had the cameras way back behind glass, so you couldn't see them, mic'd everybody, and went and shot. There wasn't even that much rehearsal, really. It was mostly about making sure you had the right actors, knowing exactly what it is you want to talk about, and going in and shooting specifically what you need.

**GH:** We did a pretty extensive amount of testing to come up with what we finally came up with. And we'd just come off of doing a couple of series for HBO called *Unscripted* and *K Street*, so that was actually a school for us on the way that George wanted this to work. He wanted it to feel not self-conscious. He wanted it to feel like things were just being caught, as opposed to staging beautiful tableaux and that kind of stuff. Thematically, it fit because—and I never really thought about it this way—you gather news footage sort of on the fly. And in a way, I think that's how this feels.

*How did using the archival footage affect the structure of the story?*
**GH:** It definitely affected the structure, because you're also limited to what you have. We knew that we wanted to use these five episodes, so as we started to look at it, we started to see what the most compelling parts of those pieces were, and how some of it mattered, some of it didn't, and what worked best for the scene.
**GC:** Sometimes we'd go to something like *Point of Order*, the documentary about the Army-McCarthy hearing, and we'd see this piece of footage where McCarthy is ranting and raving. Then there's a shot of everybody getting up and leaving while he's still ranting and raving, sort of underneath it. And it sounds like Fredric March at the end of *Inherit the Wind*. But we went back to the original footage and those were actually two different days. We realized, even as an old liberal, that that's really manipulative and that doesn't work. You can't do that. We found that a lot of times with the archival stuff, we had to go back down to the very basic archives, to the very first original footage and start from there, so that we weren't misrepresenting the truth or carrying on a misrepresentation of the truth.
**GH:** It was a hard task to get it all in order, and then actually get the footage and restore it, and all those steps along the way.

*You had to do restoration?*
**GH:** Yes, in many of those instances, the best thing we could get was a three-quarter-inch tape. Everything was gone. There was only one instance where we got actual 35mm film. Originally, they shot it all on 35mm. We didn't want to do anything digitally, in terms of putting pictures in, so we had to have it there on the set, either 35mm or

16mm, projected. So just logistically, getting all that done was sort of interesting. We decided early on that we wanted to use archived footage. We started talking about who we would ever get to play McCarthy and, as we started to have those conversations, we felt like no matter who we got, no matter how good he was, people were going to say it's over the top. The only way we could get away with McCarthy being over the top was to use the real McCarthy. So that's how we came to that decision, because nobody was going to be able to play McCarthy without getting nailed for overacting, and McCarthy does a great job himself, so we thought let's just use him. We also knew that we were never going to see McCarthy outside of the studio, the way that we don't really see any of the guys outside of work, except for Joe and Shirley.

*Right. They're also, kind of, the only emotional relationship that we see. What was their function in the story?*

**GH:** First of all, they're both alive, so they were our best conduit into that period. As we talked to them and found out they were married, but they couldn't tell anybody, we felt that was a very interesting thing. It played into this idea of secrecy, that people had to keep all these secrets, and that there was a lot of fear. I'm sure that was standard policy back then—it was just interesting to us. The purpose of that story line was to give people a glimpse of how it was affecting people in the world. The first time you see them, the first scene, they're fearful about signing this thing, and what it means and who's going to hear them and all that stuff. We also put that scene in, at night when they were in bed, to show that everything wasn't cut-and-dry, black and white. It's easy in hindsight to say, McCarthy was wrong and bad and all that, but at the time, people, I think, were probably a little more ambivalent.

*You followed them home, but never had a private moment with Murrow.*

**GC:** We just decided that that wasn't what the story was. From the very beginning, that was never going to be the story. We thought, because Joe and Shirley were our consultants and they'd given us some really interesting stuff to play on, we thought, Okay, if we want to play with a secondary character in the story. But I didn't want to hear what the major characters felt. I didn't want Fred Friendly to go home to his wife and go, "Gee, this is scary stuff." I also didn't want anybody to feel like they were completely right. That's why we had that scene with Joe and Shirley, where he says, "What if we're wrong?" In history we could look at it with hindsight and go, "Of course they were right, that's an easy one." But at the time, I bet it was a little trickier and a little scarier.

It's exactly the same thing as now with these detainees in Guantánamo Bay. You say, Okay, either they're prisoners of war and they get Geneva Convention rights or they're criminals and they get the right to face their accuser in a speedy trial. Now, having said all that, and fighting that fight, at the end of the day you go, Yeah, but what happens if Padilla actually has a dirty bomb and wants to set it off? The questions are more complex than just good and bad, and we didn't have answers for it, we just had questions. But we knew that ultimately—and this is why Murrow lasted as long as he did—Murrow's answers were always constitutional. He didn't ever claim that Annie Lee Moss was or wasn't a Communist. But the union will not survive if we give away what we fought over, to separate ourselves from King George. We don't make it if we toss away all the civil liberties that we fought so hard for. Then what are we preserving?

*There's a great deal of journalism involved in just telling this story.*
**GC:** Yeah, there is. If you get any facts at all wrong in your story, a group of people will come out and go, "You got it wrong!" Sort of, "You got this one piece wrong, so it's all bullshit." And then you marginalize the whole thing. So Grant and I were very careful to do exactly what good journalists have always done, and what I learned from a long time back, which is to double-source *everything*; at least two sources on every single scene in the movie. We wrote the dialogue, we arranged the story, but some of the dialogue was taken. Murrow did say, "The fear is in the room." And Paley did say, "I don't want to have a stomachache every time you take on a controversial subject." But he didn't ask Murrow about Alger Hiss. We thought that was a good place to land that story, so that you could raise the argument that Murrow was editorializing.

*How did you work toward the major conflict?*

**GH:** Well, it sort of builds. There are segments. It's, "When are we going to go after McCarthy?" Then, "Okay, we're going to go after McCarthy. Okay, we went after him. Now what's going to be the fall-out?" Then, "Here's the fallout, and how do we address it?" So there are these incremental steps. The central conflict, obviously, is between Murrow and McCarthy, though it doesn't play out in a real traditional way.

*Tell me more about weaving the idea of fear into the story, because the threat is mostly offscreen.*

**GC:** Well, it's a fairly easy thing to do. Actually, it's not a fairly easy thing to do, but it's a much easier thing to do inside a room than it is out. The first thing we had was this claustrophobia. If you look at all those old *Twilight Zones*, or old movies like *Dracula*, they're scary because of what you *don't* see. Mostly it was because of budgetary reasons, but a lot of times it was simply, "We're not going to show you these things, but they're out there." They're the unknown. The original *The Thing*, until the monster shows up, is one of the scariest movies you've ever seen. Then the monster shows up and it's James Arness wandering around with big hands, and who gives a shit? But until he shows up, it's a scary movie because they're talking about it and they're worried about it.

To us, the beauty of it was that the problem is all around them and nobody is talking about it. But you sense it, and you get it, and you feel it. And then when the monster actually shows up, you see actual footage of Joe McCarthy accusing Edward R. Murrow of being a traitor and "the cleverest of the jackal pack." When people today, who know nothing of the story, see that actually happen with real footage, they gasp in the theater. Literally, every time I've seen it, you hear people go, "Uhh!" Take a deep breath in, because they can't believe it actually got that far.

**GH:** It's really George's directing. I remember, he would always remind me to remind him, saying, "Look, we have to keep the tension up. We have to keep that offstage fear present whenever we can, however we can." So, it could be when Joe Wershba was at the congressional hearings and gets approached by Surine—that was a real guy and that was a real scene. A lot of that dialogue was taken right from what Joe said happened—or when Joe and Shirley are in the copy room, or when Shirley's at home with Joe, and she tells about talking to Howard K. Smith in London, and looking over her shoulder to see who was listening. She makes a joke and says it was Chairman Mao or whatever, but we tried to infuse it in little moments. We were very conscious of not wanting to hit things over the head, because a film like this could become preachy. It could become didactic. It could become a drag. So we were very conscious of trying to be subtle.

*George, the two films you've directed,* Confessions *and* Good Night, and Good Luck, *have both been about television, television personalities, where television can be great and where it utterly fails. This is obviously something that occupies you.*
**GC:** Well, it's something I know a lot about. I grew up in it and spent my whole life in it. My father's in it and it's a big part of my life. So, I think you direct and write about things you know, first. Second, I like television in a lot of ways, and I think it has great promise. I think I sort of worked backwards; I started with a movie that's basically about the beginning of the downfall of television. And then I go do a movie that's basically about when television did it exactly the way it should do it. I guess I'll do radio next.

*A question you raise, which is particularly prescient now, is of the role of the journalist. Now, under that banner within television journalism, we have reporters, investigative reporters, pundits, anchors, even entertainers. They don't all seem to have the same responsibilities, and I believe that's led to a good deal of confusion and distrust within the public of journalism as a whole. The expectation of impartiality or objectivity, if any ever actually existed, seems diminished, and Murrow taking on McCarthy seems to have contributed to that state. How did you approach that issue, and how did Murrow?*
**GH:** This is the age-old question and the can of worms that Murrow opened up; he did editorialize. He talks about it. He and Friendly felt that there was one right side to that story, but the problem is that

everybody's not Murrow. So he did open up the world for the Bill O'Reillys and all the rest in the world. There is a discussion to be had about that, but for our purposes in this film, we weren't arguing that. We were illuminating that. It's really for the audience to decide what this has become. I mean, if you look at a Ted Koppel, you never know what side he's on. You just think that he is questioning and looking for whoever is wrong. I think that an investigative journalist has an agenda, and the agenda is to illuminate the truth, and truth can be world-changing. I mean, the reporters who cracked Watergate changed the course of America. And the ramifications are still apparent today to me.

*Funny you should mention, because this month* Nightline *is being reformatted without Ted Koppel, turning it into a newsmagazine probably not much different than all the others. After that, what's left but* 60 Minutes *and* NewsHour with Jim Lehrer?

**GC:** I think the press will come back. I think it's having a renaissance now, after Hurricane Katrina. Sooner or later they grow their gonads back and start to ask questions. You could argue that what Murrow did does lead to Fox News, and, in fact, O'Reilly and a couple of people made that argument, saying, "Murrow was the first advocate in the news and, if you want that advocate, then why am I wrong?" In the same way that Cronkite did when he came back from Vietnam and said, "This is failed policy and it didn't work," and it was the turning point in the war, I would argue that taking sides, in general, should be against power. The idea is that power has the microphone and can get it anytime it wants. The idea behind taking up a side is to say, Listen, here's a voice that doesn't get heard or isn't heard enough. Generally, that's against any power. My father went directly at Jimmy Carter when the OPEC nations raised the price of gas. He went directly at Gerald Ford when he pardoned Nixon. It was about questioning authority. Because, as we know, if you don't question authority, if you don't question power, it corrupts, always. We have a history of it from the beginning of time. So is it frightening now, what passes for journalism on television? Sure. But there's also some great reporting going on out there.

I'm an optimist. I happen to think we go through waves. Every thirty years we panic, and we round up all the Japanese Americans and put them in internment camps after Pearl Harbor, or something. And then we figure ourselves out. The beauty of our country is we're actually good at fixing them, and it's a process always led by journalists. They led the Civil Rights movement. They led the Women's Rights movement. With the New Deal, the Great Society, the space program, the press led the way. So, I actually have faith in it. Will there always be advocates of the government? Of course there will. That's always existed, but it's now turned into what magazines and newspapers have been in the past, where you go to the place that best represents your political and social view. If you're conservative, you go to Fox. If you're a liberal, maybe you watch CNN or ABC or whatever it is, NPR. But at the end of the day what happens is, we're starting with a different fact basis. If you talk to my aunt and uncle, the reason we're in Iraq is because of 9/11 and we have to get the guy who got us in 9/11. Because they got their facts directly from the world that they believe in. So we have to get past this point of polarization to where people start asking more questions, and I think we will. I think the idea that a president who was as popular as Bush can be down to 37 percent popularity today in a *Wall Street Journal* poll—which is certainly not a liberal paper—tells you that people are actually getting sick of hearing sugar-coated shit, and want to hear the truth. I think we're cyclical that way.

Good Night, and Good Luck *is, in some ways, a buddy picture between Friendly and Murrow. Did your relationship with Grant inform the way you wrote the characters?*
**GH:** I think our group of friends, and the way that our group interacts, informed us on how to write that group of guys, more than anything. The language was different, the subject was different, but there's a way that guys talk to each other. There's a way they joke. There's a way they deflect that was informed by our friendships.
**GC:** You know, Grant and I are best friends for twenty-three years. He loaned me $100 to get headshots in 1982 for a *Joanie Loves Chachi* audition. We talk every day. We play basketball on Sundays together.

His brother and I are really close, and certainly that has a huge effect on how the characters are written. Remember, I grew up in the newsroom and watched these guys, all with that same dark sense of humor, that I thought it should represent what my friends do. I've got the greatest friends in the world. They're the kind of guys who rise to the occasion, and you're either the guy you want batting in the ninth inning with two men out or you're not. And all these guys, you want them batting in the ninth inning.

---

**Rob Feld** is a writer and independent producer at Manifesto Films. His writings on film and interviews with such noted filmmakers as James L. Brooks, Charlie Kaufman, Bill Condon, Peter Hedges, John Turturro, Spike Jonze, Peter Jackson, David O. Russell, Darren Aronofsky, Alexander Payne, Woody Allen, David Hare, David Koepp, Shari Springer Berman, Robert Pulcini, Dan Futterman, and Bennett Miller appear regularly in *Written By* magazine and *DGA Magazine*, as well as in the Newmarket Shooting Script® series.

Good Night, And Good Luck.

by

George Clooney
&
Grant Heslov

March 2, 2005
PRODUCTION DRAFT

1      INT. CHICAGO HOTEL - BALLROOM AND STAGE - NIGHT     1

October 15, 1958. The Radio and Television News Directors Association Annual meeting.

We're in the wings of the Stage. Standing there alone is Edward R. Murrow. He looks slightly ill at ease. He lights a cigarette... he looks at some notes in his hand as we overhear his glowing introduction by SIG MICKELSON, an executive at CBS

> MICKELSON
> ...In 1935 Ed Murrow began his career with CBS. When World War II broke out, it was his voice that brought the Battle of Britain home to us through his "This Is London" radio series. He started with us all...many of us here tonight...when television was in its infancy, with the news documentary show, "See it Now." And he threw stones at giants. Segregation, exploitation of migrant workers, apartheid, J. Edgar Hoover, not the least of which, his historical fight with Senator McCarthy. He is the host of our enormously popular show "Person to Person" and tonight he is here with his son Casey, wife Janet, and all of you who he's worked with...inspired... lectured...taught. Ladies and gentlemen, the Radio-Television News Directors' Association and Foundation welcomes Mr. Edward R. Murrow.

Cheers and applause as we walk with him to the podium.

A long awkward pause.

> MURROW
> This might just do nobody any good. At the end of this discourse a few people may accuse this reporter of fouling his own comfortable nest, and your organization may be accused of having given hospitality to heretical and even dangerous thoughts.

CUT TO:

(CONTINUED)

1      CONTINUED:                                                    1

Close ups of people listening.  Smiling.  Not aware that
this is not to be the comfortable acceptance speech you
might hear of a retiring employee getting his gold watch.
This will become what will later be called "The Box of
Lights and Wires Speech."  One of THE MOST IMPORTANT
broadcast journalism speeches EVER.  It is an attack on
everyone in this room... an attack on himself.  And, at
this point, it has just begun.

                         MURROW (CONT'D)
              But the elaborate structure of
              Networks, Advertising Agencies and
              Sponsors will not be shaken or
              altered.  It is my desire, if not
              my duty, to try to talk to you
              journeymen with some candor about
              what is happening to radio and
              television.  If what I have to say
              is responsible, then I alone am
              responsible for the saying of it.
              Our history will be what we make
              of it. And if there are any
              historians about fifty or a
              hundred years from now, and there
              should be preserved the Kinescopes
              for one week of all three
              networks, they will there find
              recorded in black and white, or
              color, evidence of decadence...
              escapism, and insulation from the
              realities of the world in which we
              live. We are currently wealthy,
              fat, comfortable and complacent.
              We have a built in allergy to
              unpleasant or disturbing
              information. Our mass media
              reflect this. But unless we get up
              off our fat surpluses and
              recognize that television in the
              main is being used to distract,
              delude, amuse and insulate us,
              then television and those who
              finance it, those who look at it
              and those who work at it, may see
              a totally different picture too
              late.

                                                          CUT TO:

                                                      (CONTINUED)

1    CONTINUED: (2)                                    1

Over black we read:   **"The little picture"**


2    INT. NEWSROOM                                     2

Our story starts in a busy TV newsroom.  The CBS Newsroom
to be exact.  The year is 1953.  We're following a young
female, NATALIE, as she carries a tray with six cups of
coffee.  For the next few moments she'll give us a tour
of the newsroom.  Secretaries typing.  The AP and UP wire
clicking away.  A camera crew runs by.  A reporter, JOHN
AARON, with several cans of film stops us.

                    AARON
            Natalie, this is the Stevenson
            footage from yesterday...

        NATALIE                          AARON
Okay. I'll give it to Leo.       ...Charlie wanted me to get
How many cans is it?             it...what?  Oh.


                                 It's two cans.  There's
                                 some notes that go with it
Fred's in with the guys,         for Fred.
you can't go in...

                    NATALIE
            I'll get the notes to Fred and you
            can go ahead and give the film to
            Leo.

        NATALIE (CONT'D)                     AARON
He's in projection...            In the projection room?
yes, the projection room.        Okay.  Thanks, Natalie.
Thanks John.

We now follow AARON as NATALIE heads down the corridor.
AARON stops in the copier room where a mimeograph machine
is rolling out copies.  There is also coffee in the room
which is why AARON has stopped in.  Off to one corner
SHIRLEY is filing folders while JOE WERSHBA is making
copies at the mimeograph.

                    AARON
            Hey, Joe.  Shirley.  What's going
            on in here?  (Teasing)  Just
            making sure.  Two attractive
            people alone in the copy room...

        WERSHBA                          AARON
        (kidding)                I mean...I certainly won't
Okay, John, you caught us.       say anything...
But don't tell anyone...

                                    (CONTINUED)

> SHIRLEY
> (also kidding)
> Well don't tell Paley... he'll
> fire me.

> WERSHBA
> ...Both of us, Shirley.

> AARON
> I think Joe would get the axe...

AARON finishes getting his coffee.

> AARON
> Well, rules are made to be broken.

> WERSHBA                    SHIRLEY
> I think he's right,          (To Ed)
> Shirley. What'ya say we    You can afford to say that.
> grab a drink tonight...

> WERSHBA
> It might be good for you to get
> out a little.

Shirley smiles.

> AARON
> Just a couple of guys trying to
> help.

As AARON leaves.

> SHIRLEY
> The day I need dating advice from
> you two knuckleheads is the...

We hear AARON laughing down the hall. We stay on Joe and
Shirley who just stare at each other in silence. Then
the mood suddenly becomes more serious.

> SHIRLEY (CONT'D)
> Let me see this, I don't know...

He hands her a concealed paper.

> WERSHBA
> It's simply a "Loyalty Oath."
> There's nothing in it about...

> SHIRLEY
> To CBS?

(CONTINUED)

CONTINUED: (2)

                    WERSHBA                          SHIRLEY
To America...                              ...You promise to be a
                                           loyal American?
... All the reporters have
it.  Fred signed it...                     Who are you promising this
                                           to?  CBS?...Paley?
Murrow too... Murrow signed
it.                                        Murrow signed it?

They sit and look at each other.  She reads it again.

                    WERSHBA                          SHIRLEY
...I've had it for a while,                     (Reading)
I thought it was a joke at              "Are you now or have you
first but... there's a lot              ever been a member of these
of pressure... I don't                  organizations that appeared
know.                                   on the Attorney General's
                                        list of subversive groups."

                         SHIRLEY (CONT'D)
                    Alright, let's think about it.
                    What is it really saying... is it
                    a civil liberties issue?  Is it
                    censorship?

                         WERSHBA
                    I don't know.  Is it simply
                    stating for CBS that I'm not a
                    communist?

                         SHIRLEY
                    Murrow signed it?

            WERSHBA                          SHIRLEY
And Fred... and Stanton.            Maybe you should talk to
                                    Murrow...

                         SHIRLEY (CONT'D)
                    If you don't sign it, are you and
                    I a target?

                         WERSHBA
                    If I don't sign it, they'll fire
                    me.

Shirley leans over, puts her hand on top of his and gives
him a quick kiss.

                         SHIRLEY
                    Well at least then we can tell
                    everyone the truth...

                                                    (CONTINUED)

2      CONTINUED: (3)                                    2

As she exits.

                                                CUT TO:

3      INT. SCREENING ROOM - DAY, 1953                3

We fade up. It's fairly dark. Projected on the wall is footage of MCCARTHY being introduced by MR. KEEFE.

In the foreground - silhouetted, are several of the greatest newsmen of their generation... but they don't know it yet. PALMER WILLIAMS - EDDIE SCOTT - JESSE ZOUSMER - FRED FRIENDLY - DON HEWITT - JOE WERSHBA - JOHN AARON - CHARLIE MACK - all young.

They are to become known as "Murrow's Team" and this room is the place where the standard for broadcast journalism will be founded.

Quietly seated in the very back is MURROW.

As they look on we see the footage.

                            MR. KEEFE
Well, you'd sometimes think to hear the quartet that call themselves "Operation Truth" damning Joe McCarthy and resorting to the vilest smears I've ever heard. Well? This is the answer. And if I could express it in what's in my heart right now, I'd do it in the terms of the poet who once said: "Ah, 'tis but a dainty flower I bring to you. Yes, 'tis but a violet, glistening with dew. But still in its heart there lies beauties concealed. So in our heart, our love for you lies unrevealed."

                            MCCARTHY
You know, I used to-- pride myself on the idea that I was a bit tough, especially over the past eighteen or nineteen months, and we've been kicked around then bullwhipped and damned. (tearing up) I didn't think that-- I could be touched very deeply. But tonight, frankly, my cup and my heart is so full I can't talk to you.

                                        (CONTINUED)

FRIENDLY
Leo, that's enough, turn it off.

ZOUSMER                          WERSHBA
What poet was that?              'Tis but a dainty flower I
                                 bring to you.

ZOUSMER                          SCOTT
No... Hey, Don, who wrote        There was a young man from
that?                            Nantucket...

AARONS                           FRIENDLY
I believe it was Roy             Did you see that... I just
Cohn...                          like it because McCarthy's
                                 crying.

ZOUSMER                          SCOTT
It's funny.  I didn't think      Something, something...
it's all that damning...         BUCKET.
but it is funny.

FRIENDLY                         AARON
No, there's nothing really.      We'll cut it down - Joe,
But it sure is fun to see        we'll make it shorter.
the Junior Senator
wallowing.

WERSHBA
Yeah, we'll cut it down.  Just for
the files.

MURROW sits there head down, cigarette dangling from his
lip.

FRIENDLY                         ZOUSMER
Okay file it, we might use       Hey, did you hear the
it later... a piece about        latest polls?  The most
poetry or something...           trusted man in America is
                                 Milton Berle.

SCOTT
Hey Ed... what rhymes with bucket?

They all smile.

There is a long pause.

MURROW
... Pail.

FRIENDLY
Okay fellas... keep looking.  File
that Joe, you and Millie cut it
down to a minute...

                                              (CONTINUED)

3    CONTINUED: (2)                                           3

They all start to leave.

                    WERSHBA
                   (To Murrow)
          I saw Charles Laughton in the
          green room... is he on the show
          tonight?

                    MURROW
          Tonight's Person to Person will be
          an "At Home" piece with J. Edgar
          Hoover and Roy Cohn...

They all laugh.

                    MURROW (CONT'D)
          Vacuuming, making dinner.

          SCOTT                        WERSHBA
     ...Raising kids.          But, what's Roy doing?

As they exit, JOHN AARON approaches FRIENDLY.

                    AARON
          Fred, did you guys look at the
          Secretary Stevens stuff?  It's
          great.

          FRIENDLY                     MURROW
     We will, John.          Not yet.

                    AARON (CONT'D)
          Just watch it till the end... he's
          really good on camera...

                    MURROW
          Okay, John.

                    AARON
          All the way to the end; it's worth
          it.

                    MURROW
          Thanks, John.

AARON exits.

MURROW and FRIENDLY remain in the room.  MURROW seated,
FRIENDLY standing by the door.

                    FRIENDLY
          It's pretty good stuff, Ed.

                                          (CONTINUED)

                        MURROW
            You ever spent any time in
            Detroit?

                        FRIENDLY
            We've got twenty or so of these
            pieces filed, we could use a
            couple...

                        MURROW
            There's a story here in the
            Detroit Free Press ... Dexter,
            Michigan... a kid named Milo
            Radulovich...

                        FRIENDLY
            Italian?

                        MURROW
            Irish... Air Force kicked him out
            because his dad read some Serbian
            newspaper... they call Milo a
            security risk.

                        FRIENDLY
            Is his dad a communist?  Who
            brought the charges?

                        MURROW
            I don't know... the Air Force...
            the charges were in a sealed
            envelope, nobody saw them...

                        FRIENDLY
            Not even at the hearing?

                        MURROW
            He was declared guilty without a
            trial and told if he wanted to
            keep his job he'd have to denounce
            his father and his sister... so he
            told 'em to take a hike.

                        FRIENDLY
            His sister?

                        MURROW
            Let's send Joe and Charlie down
            there, see if he's any good on
            camera...

                        FRIENDLY
            Is he being brought before the
            committee?

                                        (CONTINUED)

3       CONTINUED: (4)                                            3

                              MURROW
               No.

                              FRIENDLY
               So, it's not McCarthy.

                              MURROW
               Isn't it?

          FRIENDLY picks up the newspaper and reads.

                              FRIENDLY
               Milo Radulovich...

                                                    CUT TO:


4       INT. SOUND EDITING ROOM                                   4

          A close up of Milo Radulovich talking, it's projected on
          the wall from a 16mm projector.

                              MILO
               Yes, if I am being judged on my
               relatives... are my children going
               to be asked to denounce me... are
               they gonna be judged on what their
               father was labeled... are they
               going to have to explain to their
               friends etc., why their father is
               a security risk?  I see a chain
               reaction that has no end to
               anybody.

          We pull out and we're in the sound/broadcast room
          watching this on screen.  In the B.G. we see the darkened
          News set.  In the foreground sits MURROW, FRIENDLY and
          SIG MICKELSON.

          MICKELSON isn't pleased.

                              MICKELSON
               Well, that's new.  I don't think
               you can call this a neutral piece.

          MURROW                        FRIENDLY
     Sig, I think the other        We tried to talk to the Air
     side's been represented       Force, they haven't gone on
     rather well for the last      record.  Their lawyers
     couple of years if...         won't unseal the
                                    envelope...I...


                                                    (CONTINUED)

4        CONTINUED:

                        MICKELSON (CONT'D)
              So, you just want to forego the
              standards that you've stuck to for
              fifteen years... both sides... no
              commentary... I'm just making sure
              we identify what you're both
              doing.

        MURROW                              FRIENDLY
We all editorialize, it's      We're giving them the
just to what degree... I'm     information up front and
aware that... Fred, hold       asking them to explain
on... Fred...                  themselves...

                        MURROW
              I've searched my conscience and I
              can't for the life of me find any
              justification for this.  I simply
              cannot accept that there are, on
              every story, two equal and logical
              sides to an argument.  If you call
              it editorializing, then call it
              that... They'll have equal time to
              defend themselves.

                        MICKELSON
              It is editorializing. Period.  You
              understand the position you're
              putting us in?

                        FRIENDLY
              We're all in it together, if the
              Senate or...

                        MICKELSON
              Do me this favor, Fred, and avoid
              any speeches about how we're all
              in a big boat together... please
              don't insult me... I have to go
              back to Mr. Paley and to Alcoa,
              who sponsors your show <u>and</u> also
              happens to have military
              contracts, and tell them they
              might be caught in a tough bind
              because of a beef you had with Joe
              McCarthy.

                        MURROW
              We're not going at McCarthy.

                        MICKELSON
              You're starting the goddamn
              fire... I know what this is, Ed...

                                              (CONTINUED)

> MURROW
> When Bill and I talked about this,
> you - and this goes back to "Hear
> It Now" - you, agreed that
> corporate would have no influence
> on news content...

> MICKELSON
> What I'm saying is - Don't try to
> con me into thinking that this is
> good for me... just do me that
> courtesy.

A knock on the door and NATALIE, Friendly's secretary,
pokes her head in.

> NATALIE
> I'm sorry Mr. Mickelson, Mr.
> Murrow... Fred, there's a Colonel
> Anderson here to see you...

> FRIENDLY                          NATALIE
> Okay, Natalie, where is    He's in your office...
> he?... Sorry gentlemen...  there's two of them...

> FRIENDLY
> Maybe these guys love the
> transcript and are here to
> congratulate me...

They exit.

MURROW and MICKELSON just sit there smiling at one
another.

> MICKELSON
> Go after Joe Kennedy...we'll pay
> for it.

> MURROW
> I've got a great story about
> Hoover...

They both smile. Not happy smiles. Just two men
acknowledging that they've come to a crossroad that they
may not survive.

> MICKELSON
> Do you know how many "Person to
> Persons" you'll have to do to make
> this up?...

MURROW nods.

(CONTINUED)

4          CONTINUED: (3)                                    4

                         MURROW
               Judy and her daughter Liza next
               week...

                         MICKELSON
               No chance... you're interviewing
               Rin Tin Tin...

Silence.

                         MICKELSON (CONT'D)
               I'll talk to Mr. Paley... Alcoa
               won't pay for the ads... we
               probably won't either... but
               nobody will stop you.

                         MURROW
               How much are the ads?

                         MICKELSON
               Three thousand.

                         MURROW
               I'll split it with Fred...

STANTON starts to exit.

                         MURROW (CONT'D)
               He just won't have Christmas
               presents for his kids this year...

                         MICKELSON
               He's a Jew.

                         MURROW
               Don't tell Fred, he loves
               Christmas.

MICKELSON exits.

We stay on MURROW.

                                              CUT TO:


5          INT. FRED FRIENDLY'S OFFICE                       5

FRIENDLY, COLONEL ANDERSON and COLONEL JENKINS are seated
at the opposite sides of the desk.

                         ANDERSON
               ...Yes, we did... and we read the
               transcript... we've not been
               allowed to see the footage...

                                              (CONTINUED)

5          CONTINUED:                                                    5

> FRIENDLY
> We're still shooting it... Charlie
> Mack is on a plane from Dexter
> with the last of the interviews.
> We'll be going right down to the
> wire.

> ANDERSON
> Your show airs tomorrow... how can
> we possibly have time to approve
> and check the story that you are
> running in the limited amount of
> time you've given us?

> FRIENDLY
> Colonel, with all due respect you
> have been invited to <u>participate</u>
> in this piece... not to <u>approve</u>
> this piece. We're going with the
> story that says that the US Air
> Force tried Milo Radulovich
> without one shred of evidence and
> found him guilty of being a
> security risk... without the
> Constitutional right to...

> ANDERSON
> And, you, who also have not seen
> the evidence, are claiming he's
> not a security risk... wouldn't
> you guess that the people who <u>have</u>
> seen the contents of that envelope
> might know a little more about
> what makes someone a danger to his
> country?... or, do you think it
> should just be you that
> decides?...

> FRIENDLY
> Who are these "people"?... Are
> they elected... appointed... Do
> they have an axe to grind?... Is
> it you, sir... or Colonel Jenkins?
> Do you know the contents of that
> sealed envelope?...

They sit there very still.

> JENKINS
> Mr. Friendly. We have been a
> friend and an ally of both Mr.
> Murrow and CBS News. The story
> that you are going to run tomorrow
> is without merit.
>                    (MORE)

                                              (CONTINUED)

5     CONTINUED: (2)                       5

                         JENKINS (CONT'D)
So before you take the steps that
cannot be undone, I urge you to
reconsider your stand.  These are
very dangerous waters that you are
attempting to navigate.

We watch Friendly as he weighs this information.

                                   CUT TO:

6     INT. EDITING ROOM ONE                   6

Tight on a monitor, Milo Radulovich's lawyer is talking.
(This will be the real footage.)  Beneath him, on the
screen the subtitles read, **October 20, 1953.**

                         LAWYER
The Air Force did not produce a
single witness, we were not told
who the accusers were.  We had no
right to confront them or cross
examine them... But at the
conclusion of the trial, although
we had met the allegations, the
Air Force made findings at the
conclusion of the hearing that
every single allegation was true.
As a matter of fact we have had no
hearing at all, we have had no day
in court.  In all the thirty-two
years that I have been a
practicing attorney in Detroit, I
have never witnessed such a farce
and travesty upon justice as this
thing has developed.

The subtitles fade, the image stops and begins to run
backwards.

Another subtitle comes up. **Five minutes to air.**

We pull back and see we're in the editing bay, SCOTT is
hopping from one foot to the other.  People are
scrambling.

          SCOTT                     MILLIE
Damnit Millie, unload this       A couple more seconds...Is
thing before I crack...          Don ready for this?...Tell
                              him I front loaded the
I'll tell Don...five              opening for about five
seconds...front loaded...     seconds extra...

SCOTT gets the film and takes off sprinting down the hall
yelling.

                                (CONTINUED)

6    CONTINUED:                                                  6

> SCOTT
> OUT OF THE WAY... NATALIE...
> NATALIE, tell Joe he's gonna have
> to do the voice over live we
> didn't get time to sync it up...

NATALIE enters the hall running with him.

> SCOTT
> I need a booth with a live
> mic...

> NATALIE
> Joe's on the set... you
> tell him... I'll get the
> booth set...

FRIENDLY enters the control room, it's a mad house of
preparation.

> FRIENDLY
> Don, it's front loaded for
> about five seconds and it's
> missing the voice-over for
> the last piece... Joe can
> do it live so we need you
> to open a booth...

> HEWITT
> How much? Five seconds...
> THAT'S TOO MUCH, okay.
> Which piece is Joe gonna do
> live?... Why don't we try
> to synch it up with the
> whole show on air...?

Friendly looks at the clock.

> FRIENDLY
> I HATE THIS!

> HEWITT
> You love it. Fred, did you
> time Ed's intro? I think
> we're gonna be long...

As FRIENDLY walks into the newsroom, he shouts back.

> FRIENDLY
> Long is good... Don,
> remember no commercial
> break...

> HEWITT
> Right, right... I've got to
> add two minutes.

As WERSHBA enters, FRIENDLY heads to the set. We stay
with him as we hear WERSHBA and HEWITT.

> WERSHBA
> Don, they're doing a commercial in
> the booth...you want me to do it
> in the control room?

> HEWITT
> What commercial? We didn't have
> any commercial! Yeah, Eddie set
> up a mic... No, no wait, what am I
> thinking?... Get that idiot out of
> the booth... Joe, it's too loud in
> here...

(CONTINUED)

CONTINUED: (2)

FRIENDLY arrives on the set and there sits MURROW.

We hear "thirty seconds" over the loudspeaker.

Everywhere around, there is chaos... but, right there on
the set around MURROW is perfect calm.  He just reads his
notes, never looking up.

                    FRIENDLY
          We got the film...

                    MURROW
          Will it be ready?

                    FRIENDLY
          Yep.

FRIENDLY lights ED'S cigarette.

                    MURROW
          Funny thing, Freddy...

"Twenty seconds" over the loudspeaker.

                    MURROW (CONT'D)
          Every time you light a cigarette
          for me I know you're lying.

                    FRIENDLY
          We'll have it.

                    MURROW
          You know it occurs to me that we
          might not get away with this one.

They both smile.

"Ten Seconds" over the loudspeaker.

FRIENDLY walks over by the camera, he kneels on one knee.

MURROW sits in silence... for what seems like hours.

The STAGE MANAGER breaks the silence.

                    STAGE MANAGER
          In five... four... three... two...

He points to MURROW.

(CONTINUED)

6        CONTINUED: (3)                                    6

We cut to a TV monitor as MURROW looks up and directly
into the camera.

> MURROW
> Good evening.  A few weeks ago
> there occurred a few obscure
> notices in the newspapers about a
> Lieutenant, Milo Radulovich, a
> Lieutenant in the Air Force
> Reserves.

As MURROW continues to speak, we see the show from
different perspectives.  The monitor, the control room,
the set... MURROW'S POV.

> MURROW (CONT'D)
> And, also something about Air
> Force regulation thirty five dash
> sixty two.  That is a regulation
> which states that a man may be
> regarded as a security risk if he
> has close and continuing
> association with communists or
> people believed to have communist
> sympathies.  Lt. Radulovich was
> asked to resign in August. He
> declined.

As MURROW continues his intro, FRIENDLY on his back
slides up to Murrow's desk with a card that reads, **Milo
piece 2:40**

> MURROW (CONT'D)
> A board was called and heard his
> case, at the end it was
> recommended that he be severed
> from the Air Force, although it
> was also stated that there was no
> question whatsoever as to the
> Lieutenant's loyalty.  We propose
> to examine, in so far as we can,
> the case of Lt. Radulovich... Our
> reporter Joe Wershba, cameraman
> Charlie Mack.

As the footage plays in the B.G., MURROW talks to
FRIENDLY.

> MURROW (CONT'D)
> What did the General tell you
> yesterday?

(CONTINUED)

6      CONTINUED: (4)                         6

>                    FRIENDLY
>           Colonel, but there were two of
>           'em...

>        MURROW                          FRIENDLY
>   That makes a General.        They weren't too pleased.

>                    MURROW
>           You're gonna get audited this
>           year.

>                    FRIENDLY
>           Not me, you.  I told them I didn't
>           want to do the piece.

>                    MURROW
>           You always were yellow.

>                    FRIENDLY
>           Better than red.

They look at the clock, it reads 10:37pm.

Under this dissolve we hear MURROW'S V.O.

>                    MURROW (V.O.)
>           This is the sister, Margaret
>           Radulovich Fishman.  She neither
>           defends nor explains her political
>           activities.

>                                        DISSOLVE TO:

7      INT. "SEE IT NOW" SET                  7

We cut back tight on the monitor, mid-show.

>                    FISHMAN
>           I feel that my activities be that
>           what they may or my own political
>           beliefs are my own private affair.
>           And, I feel that the charges
>           leveled against me and by reason
>           of which they are trying to purge
>           him from the Army are... you
>           know... just seem to me to be a
>           fantastic trend in this country.

>                    (MORE)

>                                        (CONTINUED)

7    CONTINUED:                                                    7

                                    FISHMAN (CONT'D)
                        It's a...since when can a man be
                        judged, which in effect, is what's
                        happened to him, because of the
                        alleged activities of a member of
                        his family.

Still on screen we cut to WERSHBA interviewing
RADULOVICH.

                              WERSHBA
                        I guess a lot of people must have
                        asked you from time to time,
                        wouldn't it have been a lot easier
                        for you if you'd a... well, just
                        sort of kept quiet about the whole
                        thing?... maybe resigned and
                        nobody would have known anything
                        about it... and all this trouble
                        wouldn't have come to you.

                              MILO
                        Well, yes, that's right.  I could
                        have signed a resignation... which
                        was titled "A Resignation in Lieu
                        of Elimination from the Service"
                        and this would have given me an
                        honorable discharge.  However, the
                        honorable discharge would have
                        stipulated that I have been
                        discharged because the Air Force
                        could not trust me.  In other
                        words, I had been discharged as a
                        security risk.

                              WERSHBA
                        What happens to your two children?
                        That is, your five year old and
                        your five month old in terms of
                        you?

                              MILO
                        Yes.  If I am being judged on my
                        relatives... are my children going
                        to be asked to, uh... denounce
                        me?... Are they going to be judged
                        on what their father was
                        labeled... to have to explain to
                        their friends etc. why their
                        father is a security risk... I,
                        uh,.. SEE ABSOLUTELY... THIS IS A
                        CHAIN REACTION... IF... if the
                        thing is let stand as the first
                        recommendation,

                              (MORE)
                                                        (CONTINUED)

7    CONTINUED: (2)                                          7

MILO (CONT'D)
ah... was sent out by the board,
I see a chain reaction that has no
end to anybody... for anybody...

Cut back to Murrow on the set.

MURROW
Perhaps you will permit me to read
a few sentences just at the end
because I would like to say rather
precisely what I mean.  We have
told the Air Force that we will
provide facilities for any
criticisms or corrections it
should like to make in the case of
Milo Radulovich.

CUT TO:

8    INT. HALLWAY CBS                                        8

As MURROW continues in V.O., we are tight on a clock that
reads 10:58pm.

We pan off the clock and find SIG MICKELSON, walking down
the hall towards the control room.  He quietly enters.

MURROW (V.O.)
We are unable to judge the charges
against the Lieutenant's father or
sister because neither we, nor
you, nor they, nor the lawyers,
know precisely what was contained
in that manila envelope.

CUT TO:

9    INT. "SEE IT NOW" SET                                  9

MURROW
Was it hearsay, rumor, gossip,
slander, or was it hard
ascertainable fact that could be
backed by credible witnesses?  We
do not know.  We believe the son
shall not bear the inequity of the
father.  Even though that inequity
be proved and in this case it was
not...
(MORE)

(CONTINUED)

CONTINUED:

                        MURROW  (CONT'D)
            But, we also believe that this
            case illustrates the urgent need
            for the Armed Forces to
            communicate more fully than they
            have so far done the procedures
            and regulations to be followed in
            attempting to protect national
            security and the rights of the
            individual!

FRIENDLY, laying on the floor with another card, **one
minute.**

We see MICKELSON standing just inside the door watching
MURROW.  They lock eyes.

Back on the monitor as MURROW finishes.

                        MURROW  (CONT'D)
            At the same time, whatever happens
            in this whole area of the
            relationship between the
            individual and the state, we will
            do it ourselves, it cannot be
            blamed on Malenkov or Mao Tse-Tung
            or even our allies.  And, it seems
            to us - that is, Fred Friendly and
            myself - that this is a subject
            that should be argued about
            endlessly.  Good night. And, good
            luck.

On the monitor, as a commercial comes on.

We cut to the set.  Silence.  No one moves.  They wait
five seconds until Fred says...

                        FRIENDLY
            We're out.

The place EXPLODES, cheers... slaps on the back...
FRIENDLY comes over to MURROW, the phones ring off the
hook.

                        MURROW
            Are we in for it, Fred?

FRIENDLY pointedly lights MURROW'S cigarette.

                        FRIENDLY
            I think we're fine.

They both smile.

MURROW looks up and locks eyes with MICKELSON again.

                                              (CONTINUED)

9       CONTINUED: (2)                                         9

MICKELSON exits.

                                              CUT TO:


10      INT. HALLWAY CBS                                       10

The hallway outside the "See it Now" set is empty.  An
echo of cheers as the door opens and we watch MICKELSON
walk alone through the hallway past Anchorman DON
HOLLENBECK, doing the local NY news... down to the end...
out the door...and up the elevator towards William
Paley's office.

Over black we read, **"After This They're All Gonna Be
Rough"**


11      INT. PERSON TO PERSON SET                             11

Stock footage:

A distinguished gentleman looks into camera.

                        DISTINGUISHED GENTLEMAN
                  May I tell you something about
                  yourself as a member of the
                  "Person to Person" audience.
                  Based on audience research
                  studies, you are well above
                  average in education and
                  intelligence.  Your interests are
                  wide, from world affairs and
                  science to sports and show
                  business.  And you have one
                  characteristic that's rather
                  encouraging to me and that's the
                  fact that you are not easily
                  persuaded by advertising.  Now,
                  the makers of Kent considered all
                  these characteristics when they
                  chose Mr. Murrow's program to tell
                  you about Kent.  They believe that
                  Kent's story, simple and factual
                  as it is, has the greatest appeal
                  to your kind of thinking and that
                  the taste of Kent, recognizably
                  the quality taste of premium
                  quality natural leaf tobaccos,
                  will appeal to you.  Let me say
                  then that of all leading filter
                  cigarettes, Kent filters best.
                        (MORE)


                                              (CONTINUED)

11      CONTINUED:                                               11

DISTINGUISHED GENTLEMAN (CONT'D)
Which means that you get less tars
and nicotine in Kent than in any
other leading brand.  Now, if
you'll try Kent with that in mind,
I think you'll agree with many,
many other thinking people who
have changed to Kent.  They find
that it makes good sense to smoke
Kent...and good smoking, too.

The camera swings over to Murrow.

MURROW, with cigarette in hand, talks into camera.

MURROW
Not since the silent movies and
the idols they produced has
Hollywood witnessed the sort of
pilgrimage that is going on now.
Each day, oblivious of time,
weather, and the state of the
world, sightseers head in the
direction of California's San
Fernando Valley.  For there, at
the end of the tourist line, is
Sherman Oaks and the home that
Liberace has built for himself and
his mother.  This is the front and
no one knows how many people have
seen that view.  And this is the
back of the house and that's
Liberace's bedroom.

Murrow talks to a big screen.

MURROW (CONT'D)
Good evening, Lee.

LIBERACE
Good evening, Ed.

MURROW
What are you doing?

LIBERACE
Well, I'm just dictating my weekly
syndicated newspaper column and
uh...on my trusty tape recorder
here.  I, uh...also am dictating a
book.  It's an inspirational book
I'm working on right now.

There are the awkward beats of a newsman who is
uncomfortable in his shoes and an entertainer trying to
keep the conversation going.

(CONTINUED)

11    CONTINUED: (2)                                            11

                              MURROW
                 Well, you mean in addition to
                 radio, television, records and the
                 movies, you also write?

                              LIBERACE
                 That's right.  It's one of my
                 great ambitions to be a writer.

                                                          CUT TO:


12    INT. CONTROL ROOM - MINUTES LATER                        12

Murrow is still interviewing Liberace.  We see this on
control room monitors and through the windows looking
onto the stage.

                              MURROW
                 Uh-huh.  Lee, what about you?
                 Have you given much thought to
                 getting married and eventually
                 settling down?

                              LIBERACE
                 Well, actually I have, Ed.  I've
                 given a lot of thought to marriage
                 but I don't believe in getting
                 married just for the sake of
                 getting married.  I want to some
                 day find the perfect mate and
                 settle down to what I hope will be
                 a marriage that will be blessed by
                 faith and will be a lasting union.
                 In fact, I was reading about
                 lovely young Princess Margaret and
                 she's looking for her dream man,
                 too, and I hope she finds him some
                 day.

                              MURROW
                 Have you ever met the Princess?

                              LIBERACE
                 Not as yet but I have great hopes
                 of meeting her when I go to
                 England next season.  I'm going to
                 give a concert in London and I'd
                 like to meet her very much because
                 I think we have a lot in common.
                 We have the same taste in the
                 theatre and music and besides
                 she's pretty and she's single.

                                               (CONTINUED)

12     CONTINUED:                                              12


                            MURROW
                Could we move on and see a little
                more of the house?

                                                    CUT TO:


13     INT. PERSON TO PERSON SET                         13

       A few minutes later in the interview.

                            MURROW
                Well, Lee.  Thanks very much for
                letting us come and visit you.
                It's been very pleasant.  And will
                you say good night to the rest of
                your family for us?

                            LIBERACE
                I certainly will.

                            MURROW
                Thanks a lot.

                            LIBERACE
                Thanks so much.

                            MURROW
                Good night, Lee.

                            LIBERACE
                Good night, Ed.

                            MURROW
                Next week, we'll take you to
                Beverly Hills, California, to the
                house of Mickey Rooney and his new
                bride.  Until then, good night.
                And, good luck.

       We go to credits which we will shoot live.

       MURROW just sits there.  He notices DON HOLLENBECK, the
       eleven o'clock anchor and also a friend, at the stage
       door.  He waves to Don.

       NATALIE, FRIENDLY'S secretary, approaches MURROW.

                            NATALIE
                Mr. Murrow...

       MURROW doesn't respond.


                                              (CONTINUED)

CONTINUED:

> NATALIE (CONT'D)
> ...um... Mr. Murrow?

MURROW looks up.

> NATALIE (CONT'D)
> Dr. Stanton was wondering if you'd
> meet him for a drink?

> MURROW
> When?

> NATALIE
> Now.  He's at the Pentagon Bar.

> MURROW
> I can't, what the hell's he doing
> there? Just... call him, Natalie.

> NATALIE
> I'll let him know.

As she exits we follow MURROW to DON.  They walk.

> HOLLENBECK
> You're getting good at this, Ed...
> they're gonna think you like it.

> MURROW
> It pays the bills... How are you
> Don?...

> HOLLENBECK
> It's day to day...

> MURROW
> Well, if she saw how good you look
> right now... she'd be back...

> HOLLENBECK
> Tell her that if you see her...
> will you?

> MURROW
> I read the O'Brian piece.

> HOLLENBECK
> Yeah pretty tough... I'm a pinko,
> I slant the news... I'm just
> waiting for him to say my wife
> left me too...

> MURROW
> Nobody worth their salt reads him.

(CONTINUED)

13    CONTINUED: (2)                                    13

                         HOLLENBECK
            You read him.

                         MURROW
            Well, see, now I rest my case.

They stand there silently.

                         HOLLENBECK
            Does Paley read him?

                         MURROW
            Bill Paley's not going to do
            anything Don.

                         HOLLENBECK
            Listen, Ed, thanks... I came down
            here because I wanted to tell you
            how great the Lieutenant piece
            was.

                         MURROW
            Thanks.

                         HOLLENBECK
            How's the fallout?

                         MURROW
            Mostly good, surprisingly.

                         HOLLENBECK
            Is this the start?  Are you taking
            sides?

                         MURROW
            It's just a little poke with a
            stick, see what happens.

                         HOLLENBECK
            Well, let me know if I can help.

They start to walk out of the sound stage.

                         MURROW
            But you're a pinko, Don.

                         HOLLENBECK
            See you, Ed.

                                              CUT TO:

14    INT. CORRIDOR OUTSIDE SENATE CAUCUS ROOM - WASHINGTON DC14

JOE WERSHBA and his camera man CHARLIE MACK are walking
down the Senate corridor.  Charlie carries the camera,
Joe has an armload of papers and a few cans of film.

As they walk towards us DON SURINE walks into frame, his
back to us, semi blocking our view of Joe and Charlie.

                    SURINE
          Hey, Joe, what's all this Radwich
          junk you're putting out.

                    WERSHBA
          Don, I don't have time to talk to
          you now... I've got to get this
          film off to New York.

                    SURINE
          What would you say if I told you
          that Murrow was on the Soviet
          payroll in 1935?

This statement stops both Joe and Charlie cold.

They just stare at Don.

                    WERSHBA
          Give us a second will ya, Charlie.

                    MACK
          Sure.  I'll set up outside.
               (over his shoulder)
          Joe, you want just McCarthy or do
          I get Kennedy and Cohn?

                    WERSHBA
          Might as well get them all.

Charlie exits.

                    WERSHBA (CONT'D)
               (to Surine)
          Is McCarthy going to the
          Eisenhower dinner?

                    SURINE
          No idea, I don't keep the
          Senator's calender for him Joe.

                    WERSHBA
          Really?

                                        (CONTINUED)

14      CONTINUED:                                                        14

The two look at each other.  Surine then pulls out a
manila envelope with the infamous HUAC red stamp on the
outside.

He hands it to Joe who opens it.

> WERSHBA (CONT'D)
> Haven't you ever seen any spy
> films Donald?  You don't just hand
> me a classified folder.  You slip
> it into my briefcase when I'm not
> looking.

> SURINE
> It's actually perfect.  I didn't
> know who to give this information
> to, Paley or Murrow.  As you can
> imagine, Fred and I aren't very
> friendly... no pun intended.

> WERSHBA
> No pun elocuted.

As Joe reads.

> SURINE
> Elocuted.  Is that a word or did
> you just make that up?  You boys
> and your words... is Ed in New
> York right now, memorizing a
> thesaurus?

Joe continues to read.

> SURINE (CONT'D)
> Joe, what's another word for
> thesaurus?

> WERSHBA
> It must be awfully quiet at the
> Algonquin now that you're gone.

> SURINE
> Except for Harpo talking away.

Joe looks up from reading.

> WERSHBA
> What have you got, Donald?

> SURINE
> In short?  Ed Murrow has been a
> communist sympathizer since the
> 1930's.
> (MORE)

                                        (CONTINUED)

14    CONTINUED: (2)                                              14

                              SURINE (CONT'D)
                    Member of the International
                    Workers, sponsor of educational
                    trips to Moscow... and on the
                    Soviet payroll in 1934... it's all
                    there.

                              WERSHBA
                    You want to know why that's not
                    possible?  Why you would lose this
                    one, Donald?  Because everyone in
                    the country knows that, if nothing
                    else, Ed Murrow is a loyal
                    American... a patriot.

Surine smiles.

Then...

                              SURINE
                    Did you know that the word
                    gullible isn't in the dictionary,
                    Joe?

                              WERSHBA
                         (holding up the
                           folder)
                    Can I give this to Ed?

                              SURINE
                    I'd like you to.  I have copies...

                              WERSHBA
                    I think you guys go too far.

He starts to leave.

                              SURINE
                    Well if it walks like a duck and
                    talks like a duck... it's a
                    terrible shame, Murrow's brother
                    being a General in the Air Force.

As Wershba exits.

                                                            CUT TO:


15    INT. OUTER OFFICE OF WILLIAM PALEY                          15

MURROW sits waiting, he holds SURINE'S folder which reads
"Confidential" in big red letters.

Time ticks away.  This is the only man in America that
can keep Ed Murrow waiting.

                                                        (CONTINUED)

15     CONTINUED:                                              15

        The phone rings.  Paley's secretary MARY answers.

                          MARY
                Yes, Mr. Paley.  Right away.  Yes,
                sir.  No, he hasn't called... yes
                sir, the second he calls... if
                you're in a meeting, shall I...?
                Yes, sir.  Of course, sir.

        She hangs up.

                          MARY (CONT'D)
                Mr. Murrow, Mr. Paley will see you
                now.

                          MURROW
                Thank you, Miss Mary.

        MURROW enters.

16     INT. PALEY'S OFFICE                                     16

        William Paley's office is that of a powerful man.
        Paneling, awards, citations, photos with Kings and
        Presidents.

        PALEY stands behind a high-top desk with a plush leather
        stool to lean back on.  At this moment, he's standing to
        shake his old friend's hand.  There is an ease between
        these two that few people enjoy with Mr. Paley, they've
        been through a war together.

                          PALEY
                Hello, Ed.

                          MURROW
                Bill.

                          PALEY
                Sit over here.

        He points to an arrangement of leather chairs around a
        coffee table.

        They both sit.

                          PALEY (CONT'D)
                How's Janet?  Your son?

                          MURROW
                All well Bill, thanks.  Babe?

                                              (CONTINUED)

16      CONTINUED:                                          16

                         PALEY
              Fine.  She's fine.  Her fund-
              raiser got rained on, so...

                         MURROW
              That's why I don't plan anything.

                         PALEY
              Really?  You wouldn't know.

MURROW notices that PALEY is holding the same
"Confidential" folder.

After an awkward beat.

                         MURROW
              Reading fiction?

                         PALEY
              I hope.  You tell me.

                         MURROW
              Well, we know how they're gonna
              come at us.

                         PALEY
              That's just the first shot.
              Somebody'll go down...

This sinks in.

                         PALEY (CONT'D)
              Have you checked your facts.  Are
              you on safe ground?

Beat.

                         MURROW
              I've always had this fear of
              ending up on the wrong side of
              history... "Peace in our time."

                         PALEY
              ...sure, but Chamberlain lacked
              character... and a spine... no one
              would accuse you of that.

                         MURROW
              It's time Bill.  Show our cards.

                         PALEY
              My cards.  You lose, what
              happens?... Five guys find
              themselves out of work...
                         (MORE)

                                          (CONTINUED)

16    CONTINUED: (2)                                            16

> PALEY (CONT'D)
> I'm responsible for a hell of a
> lot more than five GODDAMN
> reporters.  Let it go... McCarthy
> will self-destruct, Cohn, all of
> them.

> MURROW
> Bill you told me that corporate
> would not interfere with editorial
> - the news is to be left...

> PALEY
> I write your check.  I've put you
> in that country house.  I've put
> your son through school... and you
> should have told me about this
> before it was so far down the
> road.

He stops himself from taking this too far.

They sit there very still.

Too long.

> PALEY (CONT'D)
> We don't make the news... we
> report the news.

| MURROW | PALEY |
|---|---|
| Bill, 99% of the time he's wrong about the people he's marked as communists... | ...and if he goes too far, the senate will investigate him and we will report on that... |

| MURROW | PALEY |
|---|---|
| ..but 100% of the time he's wrong when he sidesteps people's civil liberties... | ...and what are you doing? Trying him in the press... Does he get the right to face his accuser? Ed you're deciding on this and then presenting it as fact... |

> MURROW
> How far do you want to take this?

They sit for some time, and then...

> PALEY
> Everyone of your boys are clean.
> You understand.  No ties.  If
> Aaron's mother went to a group
> theater fund-raiser in 1932...
> he's out.
>          (The intercom buzzes)
>                (MORE)

                                              (CONTINUED)

16    CONTINUED: (3)                                 16

> PALEY (CONT'D)
> Hewitt too, anyone in that room...
> Make no mistake, I will cut them
> loose. Corporate won't interfere
> with editorial... but editorial
> will not jeopardize the hundreds
> of employees of the Columbia
> Broadcasting System. If you...

The intercom buzzes again.

> PALEY (CONT'D)
> Yes?

> MARY
> Mr. Paley, Senator Symington is on
> the phone...

The two stare at each other. PALEY crosses to his phone.

> PALEY
> And, we're not advertising it.

PALEY picks up the phone.

> PALEY (CONT'D)
> Hello Stu... right... Senator, I
> have a question for you...

MURROW and he continue to stare at each other and then
MURROW exits.

CUT TO:


17    INT. CBS CORRIDOR - CONTINUOUS                17

We see MURROW walking down the corridor, we hear FRIENDLY
in V.O.

> FRIENDLY (V.O.)
> Fellas, listen... let me make it
> easier. I just need to know for
> the good of the piece... if any of
> you have any connection at all...
> read a communist newsletter...
> traveled to St. Petersburg... was
> your mother dating a socialist in
> 1922... I don't care, I just need
> to know.

CUT TO:

18      INT. FRIENDLY'S OFFICE                                18

MURROW and all his team are in there but we keep the
camera on PALMER WILLIAMS.

              WERSHBA                        SCOTT
Let's leave my mother out      I did have a fling with a
of this...                     fascist once.

              FRIENDLY                      ZOUSMER
Fellas, help me out.           That musta' been fun.
Really.

              WILLIAMS                       SCOTT
I think I should excuse        Not after the war...they
myself, Ed.                    were a little down.

                    WILLIAMS
              Ed.  I think I should excuse
              myself.

              FRIENDLY                      ZOUSMER
Christ, okay that kills us.    What is it Palmer?  Why?
Really Palmer?

                    WILLIAMS (CONT'D)
              Let me get out now.  I don't want
              to hurt us.

              FRIENDLY                      WERSHBA
Hurt us?  We can't do the      Palmer?
story.

                    WILLIAMS (CONT'D)
              My ex was... I wouldn't say she
              was a communist, but she certainly
              attended meetings.  It was before
              we were married... it never really
              came up until after we were
              divorced... it didn't matter
              then... we were all on the same
              side... I'm not telling you
              anything you don't know... The
              thing of it is somebody will find
              out... they'll hurt us with it...
              I should have told you sooner...
              I'm sorry, Ed... Fred...

They all sit there in silence.

WILLIAMS goes to leave.

                                          (CONTINUED)

> MURROW
> Sit down, Palmer.

WILLIAMS sits.  Silence.

> MURROW (CONT'D)
> If none of us ever read a book
> that was "dangerous," had a friend
> who was "different," or joined an
> organization that advocated
> "change," we would all be just the
> kind of people Joe McCarthy
> wants... we're gonna go with the
> story because the terror is right
> here in this room.

Wershba stands.

> WERSHBA
> Mr. Murrow, it's been a privilege
> to have known you and worked for
> you.

The place erupts with laughter.

> MURROW
> What do you mean "have?"

> WERSHBA
> I mean it's a privilege to know
> you...

> MURROW
> And Joe, I'd like to say the same
> about you... I'd LIKE TO...

More laughter.

> FRIENDLY
> OK, fellas, that's it.  All the
> footage we've banked.  Everything.
> Jesse, you and Joe and Charlie go
> through the HUAC hearings... Eddie
> and Palmer see what else we
> have...  any speeches he gave, or
> interviews... his own words, boys,
> that's what we need...

The dialogue fades and then as we watch the faces of the
reporters we hear McCarthy's speech start...

> MCCARTHY (V.O.)
> The issue between Republicans and
> Democrats is clearly drawn.
> (MORE)

                                                    (CONTINUED)

18      CONTINUED: (2)                                          18

                          MCCARTHY (V.O.) (CONT'D)
                     It has been deliberately drawn to
                     those who have been in charge of
                     twenty years of treason.

We pan around the room looking at the faces of Murrow's
boys.

                          MCCARTHY (V.O.) (CONT'D)
                     Now the hard fact is, those who
                     wear the label "Democrat" wear it
                     with the stain of historic
                     betrayal.

                                                        CUT TO:


19      INT. SCREENING ROOM                                    19

Tight on a monitor, we now see MCCARTHY on screen.

                          MCCARTHY (CONT'D)
                     Any man who has been given the
                     honor of being promoted to General
                     and who says, "I will protect
                     another General who protects
                     communists," is not fit to wear
                     that uniform, General...

We pull back to see EDDIE SCOTT, PALMER WILLIAMS, CHARLIE
MACK and JOE WERSHBA watching, taking notation, editing
the piece.

                          MACK
                     So, the Zwicker case was in a
                     closed hearing.

                          WERSHBA
                     ...We couldn't put a camera in
                     there...we had nothing.

          MACK                              WERSHBA
Literally, nothing. He             McCarthy is publicly
goes after a decorated             humiliating the Commanding
General... Battle of the           General at Camp Kilmer...
Bulge...                           and we don't have it.

Normandy...

...Nothing.

                          WERSHBA (CONT'D)
                     So, we follow the Junior Senator
                     to Philly,
                              (to Hewitt)
                              (MORE)

                                                   (CONTINUED)

19    CONTINUED:                                              19

                          WERSHBA (CONT'D)
              use the pan down of the Washington
              Mural.  Don, it's perfect... so,
              McCarthy gets up to speak at a
              Washington's birthday
              celebration... and can you believe
              it... he pulls out the goddamn
              transcript from the <u>Zwicker closed</u>
              <u>hearing</u> and he re-enacts it for
              everybody... verbatim...
                          (to Hewitt)
              use the part there where he
              cackles, it's great.

                          MACK
              And, this time fellas, we shot the
              hell out of it.

Back on McCarthy.

                          MCCARTHY
              And, wait till you hear the
              bleeding hearts scream and cry
              about our methods of trying to
              drag the truth from those who know
              or should know who've covered up a
              Fifth Amendment communist major.
              But they say, "Oh, it's alright to
              uncover them but don't get too
              rough doing it, McCarthy..."

                                              CUT TO:


20    INT. EDITING ROOM TWO                                  20

MILLIE LERNER rushes up to JESSE ZOUSMER with two
cannisters of film.  Over this we hear SECRETARY STEVENS.

                          SECRETARY STEVENS (V.O.)
              I shall never accede to the abuse
              of Army personnel, under any
              circumstances, including committee
              hearings.  I shall not accede to
              them being brow beaten or
              humiliated.

We go to the Moviola to see SECRETARY STEVENS.

                          SECRETARY STEVENS (CONT'D)
              In light of those assurances,
              although I did not propose the
              cancellation of the hearing, I
              acceded to it.

                                              CUT TO:

21      INT. SCREENING ROOM                                    21

There is a lot of activity, people coming in and out,
footage being watched, work being done.  This is all in
silhouette.

Projected on the wall we see MCCARTHY going after a
writer, REED HARRIS, an official in charge of State
Department broadcasts to foreign countries.

(Note: this will play over the top of a montage of people
preparing for the show.  They're editing, taking phone
calls, having secret meetings, eating Chinese takeout,
etc.)

                    MCCARTHY
          And were you expelled from
          Columbia?

                    HARRIS
          I was suspended from classes on
          April 1st, 1932.  I was later
          reinstated, and I resigned from
          the university.

                    MCCARTHY
          And you resigned from the
          university.  Uh.  Did a Civil...
          Civil Liberties Union provide you
          with an attorney at that time?

                    HARRIS
          I had many offers of attorneys and
          one of those was from the American
          Civil Lib-- Liberties Union, yes.

                    MCCARTHY
          The question is:  "Did the Civil
          Liberties Union supply you with an
          attorney?"

                    HARRIS
          They did supply an attorney.

                    MCCARTHY
          The answer is yes?

                    HARRIS
          The answer is yes.

(CONTINUED)

                    MCCARTHY
        Uh, you know the Civil Liberties
        Union has been listed as a front
        for and doing work of the
        Communist Party.

                    HARRIS
        Mr. Chairman, this was 1932.

                    MCCARTHY
        Yeah, I know this was in 1932.  Do
        you know that they since have been
        listed as a front for, and doing
        the work of the Communist Party?

                    HARRIS
        I do not know that they have been
        listed.  So, sir, no I do not.

                    MCCARTHY
                    (Overlapping)
        You don't, you don't know they
        have been listed?

                    HARRIS
        I have heard that mentioned and or
        read that mentioned.

                    MCCARTHY
                    (Overlapping)
        I see.  Now, now you, you wrote
        a book, in 1932.  Uh, I'm going
        to ask you again, at the time you
        wrote this book, did you feel
        that professors should be given
        the right to teach sophomores
        that marriage, uh, let me quote,
        "...should be cast out of our
        civilization as antiquated and
        stupid religious phenoma--
        phenomenon."  Was that your
        feeling at the time?

                    HARRIS
        My feeling was that professors
        should have the right to express
        their considered opinions on any
        subject, whatever they were, sir.

                    MCCARTHY
        Wait, I'm going to ask you this
        question again.

                                        (CONTINUED)

>                    HARRIS
>          That includes that quotation.
>          They should have the right to
>          teach anything that came to their
>          minds as being a proper thing to
>          teach.
>
>                    MCCARTHY
>          I'm going, I'm going to make him
>          answer this.  I'm going to make
>          him answer.

We end the montage here and we're back in the screening
room.

>                    HARRIS
>          Well, I, I'll answer yes.  But,
>          but you, you put an implication on
>          it and you feature this particular
>          point out of a book which of
>          course is quite out of context,
>          does not give a proper... proper
>          impression of a book as a whole.
>          The American public doesn't get an
>          honest impression of even that
>          book, bad as it is, from what
>          you're quoting from it.
>
>                    MURROW
>          Alright Leo, turn it off.

As the projector goes off we go to MURROW and his team.

>            SCOTT                           FRIENDLY
> I like where he says,          We could cut Kennedy out
> "skillfully wringing my        and shorten the piece...
> neck."                         Joe... how much of Cohn
>                                going after this guy do we
>                                have?
>
>
>            SCOTT                           WERSHBA
> He's great.  He talks about    It wasn't Cohn as much as
> his book... it's...            McCarthy.
> funny... puts his own book
> down... says the sales were
> so "abysmal"... just great.
>
>           WILLIAMS                         ZOUSMER
> I want to read the book        Better anyway, it won't be
> now...                         that tough to show Roy as
>                                an ass...

(CONTINUED)

FRIENDLY
Yeah, maybe get somebody to
read his book, it would be
best if the guy wasn't
actually a commie... what?
Don't I think what?... Yeah
stick with Joe.

WERSHBA
Yeah, we should just stick
with the Junior Senator,
don't you think... Fred?...
don't you think... we
should stick with McCarthy?

FRIENDLY
It's pretty good, Ed...
this one holds his own...

SCOTT
Adlai Stevenson... that's
our ace in the hole...

WERSHBA
I've got Mundt at the end
of the reel... Howard...
Fred... just know that
there's good stuff at the
end of the reel.

MACK
There's more on the reel...
Joe... there's Mundt...

FRIENDLY
Okay hang on...HANG ON
GUYS...okay...

MACK
I told you to put it up
front Joe if you want Ed to
see it...

FRIENDLY
Fellas... Joe, just file
it... did you file it?... I
don't want anybody outside
this room involved... I
mean it.

WERSHBA
I'll get Mary to file it...
okay... yeah yeah.

The guys are starting to exit.

WERSHBA
Ed, if you just watch the end...
I'll get a Kinescope of it,
it's... it might be just what
we're looking for.  Really.

FRIENDLY
Okay, Joe, we'll look at it.

As the men rush to get this on the air.

MURROW
Are we gonna make it?

FRIENDLY
We lost a projector... yeah, we'll
make it...have you finished your
ending?

(CONTINUED)

21    CONTINUED: (4)                                          21

                              MURROW
                    It's Shakespeare.

                              FRIENDLY
                    Finish your ending.

                                                        CUT TO:


22    INT. BULLPEN - LATE NIGHT                              22

      The place is empty, it's dark. A long shot as we slowly
      dolly in, we find Friendly asleep at a desk.  Murrow is
      typing his closing for the show.


23    INT. JOE & SHIRLEY WERSHBA'S NY APT. - MORNING          23

      We start on Shirley as she brushes her hair in the vanity
      mirror, Joe dresses behind her.

      As Joe tells the story we stay on the worried face of
      Shirley.

                              WERSHBA
                    My argument was that if you just
                    show the images of McCarthy then
                    it won't make any difference.  If
                    you agree with him you'll hate the
                    piece, and if you don't you'll
                    love it.

                              SHIRLEY
                    Maybe they should wait till they
                    get more footage...

                              WERSHBA
                    I don't think we can take the
                    chance.  We have to hit McCarthy
                    before he comes after Ed.

                              SHIRLEY
                    They haven't gone after the Alsops
                    or Herb Block...

                              WERSHBA
                    The Alsops and Herb Block didn't
                    work for the Institute of
                    International Education in 1934.

      A pause.

      As Shirley takes off her wedding ring and puts it on a
      chain around her neck.

                                                        (CONTINUED)

CONTINUED:

> SHIRLEY
> Then I guess it's time.

She turns and looks at him to help him tie his tie.

> WERSHBA
> (smiling)
> Worried?

> SHIRLEY
> I didn't think I was. I don't
> know why... I was in the office on
> Friday... I answered the phone and
> it was Howard calling from London.
> He asked me what was going on with
> McCarthy, and before I answered
> him I turned and looked over my
> shoulder to see who was listening.

She finishes with his tie and gives him a kiss.

> WERSHBA
> And who was listening?

> SHIRLEY
> Chairman Mao...

They both smile.

> WERSHBA
> I'll see you at work.

He starts to leave.

> SHIRLEY
> Hey... your ring.

Joe stops and takes it off.

> SHIRLEY
> Name me another wife that reminds
> her husband to take off his
> wedding ring before he goes to the
> office.

> WERSHBA
> Ava Gardner.

They smile as he exits.

We stay on Shirley as she sits back down and looks at
herself in the mirror.

24     INT. CONTROL ROOM - "SEE IT NOW" STAGE     24

A commercial for ALCOA is underway, you could cut the
tension with a knife. Palmer Williams, and two engineers
line up camera shots.  On the stage MURROW, sits waiting.
Don Hewitt is at his left, Friendly lies at his feet.

                    NATALIE
I'm sorry Mr. Friendly.  Mr.
Murrow, Mr. Paley's on the line.

                    FRIENDLY
Maybe he's going to reimburse us
for the ads.

                    MURROW
You'd like that.

          FRIENDLY                        MURROW
I would like that.                   (Into phone)
                      This is Ed.

                    PALEY (V.O.)
There's a Knickerbocker game
tonight... I've got front row
seats... are you interested?

                    MURROW
                    (Smiles)
I'm a little busy bringing down
the Network tonight, Bill..

                    PALEY (V.O.)
Is that tonight?

                    MURROW
Knickerbockers you say?

                    PALEY (V.O.)
Front row.

                    MURROW
Game will be over in ten minutes.

Beat.

                    MURROW (CONT'D)
We're covered Bill.

                    PALEY (V.O.)
Alright.

Beat.

                        (CONTINUED)

24      CONTINUED:

> PALEY (CONT'D)
> I'm with you tonight, Ed... and
> I'll be with you in the morning as
> well.

> MURROW
> Thanks Bill.

MURROW hangs up the phone.

> FRIENDLY
> Thirty seconds Ed.

We watch from Friendly's POV we see Murrow's foot
tapping.

> FRIENDLY (CONT'D)
> In five...four...three...two...

Friendly then taps Murrow's leg with his pencil.

> MURROW
> Because a report on Senator
> McCarthy is by definition
> controversial, we want to say
> exactly what we mean to say and
> request your permission to read
> from a script whatever remarks
> Murrow and Friendly may make.
> If the Senator feels that we have
> done violence to his words or
> pictures and desires so to speak
> to answer himself, an opportunity
> will be afforded him on this
> program.  Our working thesis
> tonight is this quotation:  "If
> this fight against Communism has
> made a fight between America's two
> great political parties, the
> American people know that one of
> these parties will be destroyed...

> WILLIAMS
> Ready two.

The phone rings, he answers.

> WILLIAMS (CONT'D)
> No, this is not the eleven o'clock
> news try forty-four -- Operator, I
> tell you every week to shut off
> these phones.  Now please, no
> calls 'til eleven.

(CONTINUED)

24    CONTINUED: (2)                                              24

                         MURROW
              And the Republic cannot endure
              very long as a one party
              system."... We applaud that
              statement and we think Senator
              McCarthy ought to.  He said it
              seventeen months ago in Milwaukee.

                         WILLIAMS
              Take two... roll film.

We now see McCarthy on camera.

                         MCCARTHY
              The American people realize that
              this cannot be a fight between
              America's two great political
              parties.  If this fight against
              communism is made a fight against
              America's two great political
              parties the American people know
              that one of those parties will be
              destroyed and the Republic can't
              endure very long as a one party
              system.

                                                      CUT TO:


25    INT. PALEY'S OFFICE                                         25

PALEY sits watching by himself.

                         MURROW
              On one thing the Senator had been
              consistent.  Often operating as a
              one man committee, he has traveled
              far, interviewed many, terrorized
              some, accused civilian and
              military leaders of the past
              administration of a great
              conspiracy to turn over the
              country to communism.

                                                      CUT TO:


26    INT. "SEE IT NOW" SET                                       26

MURROW is seated in his chair.  On the monitor is
McCarthy.

                                                      (CONTINUED)

26    CONTINUED:    26

> MCCARTHY
> Well, may I say that I was
> extremely shocked when I heard
> that Secretary Stevens told two
> Army officers that they had to
> take part in the cover up of those
> who promoted and coddled
> communists. As I read this
> statement I thought of that
> quotation, "On what meat doth this
> our Caesar feed?"

27    INT. STAGE 44    27

DON HOLLENBECK sits at the news desk watching a monitor with great pride.

On the monitor is more footage of the REED HARRIS hearing.

> SENATOR MCCLELLAN
> Do you think this book that you
> wrote then did considerable harm?
> Its publication might have an
> adverse effect on the public by an
> expression of the views contained
> in it?

> HARRIS
> The sale of that book was so
> abysmally small, it was so
> unsuccessful, that the question of
> its influence, uh really, you can
> go back to the publisher, you'll
> see it was one of the most
> unsuccessful books ever put out.
> He's still sorry about it, just as
> I am.

> SENATOR MCCLELLAN
> Well, I think that's a compliment
> to American intelligence.

28    INT. JOE & SHIRLEY WERSHBA'S NY APT.    28

Shirley watches on the TV.

> MURROW
> The Reed Harris hearing
> demonstrates one of the Senator's
> techniques.
> (MORE)

(CONTINUED)

28    CONTINUED:                                              28

> MURROW (CONT'D)
> Twice he said, "The American Civil
> Liberties Union was listed as a
> subversive front." The Attorney
> General's list does not and never
> has listed the ACLU as subversive,
> nor does the FBI, or any other
> federal government agency. And,
> the ACLU holds in its files,
> letters of commendation from
> President Truman, President
> Eisenhower and General MacArthur.

The rest of MURROW'S speech will be intercut with close-
ups of all our players. Sitting silently at home, in the
control room, the newsroom, Paley's office, at home with
Shirley Wershba.

> MURROW (CONT'D)
> Earlier, the Senator asked, "Upon
> what meat does this our Caesar
> feed?" Had he looked three lines
> earlier in Shakespeare's "Caesar"
> he would have found this line
> which is not altogether
> inappropriate: "The fault, dear
> Brutus, is not in our stars but in
> ourselves." No one familiar with
> the history of this country can
> deny that congressional committees
> are useful. It is necessary to
> investigate before legislating,
> but the line between investigating
> and persecuting is a very fine
> one; and the Junior Senator from
> Wisconsin has stepped over it
> repeatedly. We must not confuse
> dissent with disloyalty. We must
> remember always that accusation is
> not proof and that conviction
> depends upon evidence and due
> process of law. We will not walk
> in fear, one of another. We will
> not be driven by fear into an age
> of unreason, if we dig deep in our
> history and our doctrine, and
> remember that we are not descended
> from fearful men, not from men who
> feared to write, to speak, to
> associate and to defend the causes
> that were for the moment
> unpopular. This is no time for
> men who oppose Senator McCarthy's
> methods to keep silent, or for
> those who approve.
> (MORE)

                                                (CONTINUED)

28      CONTINUED: (2)                                   28

> MURROW (CONT'D)
> We can deny our heritage and our
> history but we cannot escape
> responsibility for the result.
> We proclaim ourselves as indeed we
> are, the defenders of freedom
> wherever it continues to exist in
> the world; but we cannot defend
> freedom abroad by deserting it at
> home. The actions of the Junior
> Senator from Wisconsin have caused
> alarm and dismay amongst our
> allies abroad and given
> considerable comfort to our
> enemies. And, whose fault is
> that? Not really his. He didn't
> create this situation of fear, he
> merely exploited it, and rather
> successfully. Cassius was right.
> "The fault dear Brutus is not in
> our stars but in ourselves." Good
> night. And, good luck.

                                             CUT TO:

29      INT. "SEE IT NOW" SET                          29

MURROW looks to FRIENDLY who is lying at Murrow's feet.
They look to the control room...WILLIAMS shrugs his
shoulders.

> MURROW
> Nothing?

> FRIENDLY
> Natalie, call down and ask the
> switchboard if something's wrong.

> MURROW
> Maybe nobody watched.

They sit in silence.

An ALCOA commercial runs.

MURROW slumps back in his chair exhausted, he watches DON
HOLLENBECK on the eleven o'clock news come up on the
monitor.

                                         (CONTINUED)

29    CONTINUED:                                              29

                              HOLLENBECK
                    I don't know whether all of you
                    have seen what I just saw, but I
                    want to associate myself and this
                    program with what Ed Murrow has
                    just said, and say I have never
                    been prouder of CBS.

Still the phones are silent.  MURROW and company still
slumped in their seats.  A page pokes his head into
Studio 41.

                              CBS PAGE
                    Do you still want the calls held
                    back, Mr. Williams?

The staff breaks out in relieved laughter.

          FRIENDLY                           MURROW
     Open 'em up.                       It's the Junior Senator
                                        calling collect.

The phones start a chorus of rings all through the
studio.

FRIENDLY and MURROW look at each other.

                              FRIENDLY
                    Don't kid yourself, it's Reed
                    Harris thanking us for putting him
                    on the best-seller list.

They both light cigarettes and sit there basking in the
glorious sounds of phones ringing.

                              MURROW
                    You feel like a scotch?

                              FRIENDLY
                    I think everybody could use one.

                                                        CUT TO:

30    INT. PALEY'S OFFICE                                     30

PALEY sits behind his desk leaning back in his chair.
His head resting on the back of the chair.

The phone rings.  And keeps ringing.  Paley makes no move
to answer it.

We fade to black as the sound of the phone keeps ringing.

31      INT. PENTAGON BAR - NIGHT                       31

It's late night and our players are split up in different
booths waiting for the morning editions to come in... in
our first booth Friendly, Murrow and Hollenbeck are
seated and Shirley is standing with Joe.  Hollenbeck is
telling a story.

                    MURROW
          Hey Fred... what time is it?

                    FRIENDLY
          3:30, early editions are out now.

                    MURROW
          I'm not worried about that.

                    FRIENDLY
          No.  Of course not...
               (he looks to Shirley)
          Hey Shirl... honey, run across the
          street and pick up the early
          editions.

                    SHIRLEY
          All of them?

          FRIENDLY                    MURROW
     All of them.               Just get O'Brian.

          SHIRLEY                     MURROW
     OK, watch my drink.        That's like getting Tyrone
                                Power to watch your girl.

          WERSHBA                     FRIENDLY
     I'll go with you Shirley... Or Jackie Gleason to watch
                                your sandwich...

They watch Joe and Shirley exit the bar.

                    MURROW
               (offering Don a
                smoke)
          I'm going to have to fire Joe so
          those two can date...

                    HOLLENBECK
               (waving off the
                cigarette)
          I quit.

                                        (CONTINUED)

31      CONTINUED:                                          31

>                    MURROW
>                   (smiling)
>            Good time to quit.

                                                    CUT TO:


Aaron, Scott and Zousmer are huddled in another booth.

>                    SCOTT
>            ... yeah, but what could you do?

>                    AARON
>            Well, first we want to see if we
>            have jobs tomorrow...

>            AARON                        ZOUSMER
>     ...And IF we still have a    What's he gonna say?
>     job today then Tail Gunner
>     Joe gets to return fire.

>                    SCOTT
>            He's gonna say we're a pinko
>            organization with a leftist
>            agenda...

>            AARON                         ZOUSMER
>     We used his own words...      (a little too loud)
>     it's ... well we do have a    I'm a PINKO...
>     leftist agenda...

Silence... the room got a little too quiet.

>                    SCOTT
>            A little too loud there buddy...

>                    ZOUSMER
>            It got awfully quiet there didn't
>            it?

                                                    CUT TO:


We're back with Fred and Ed.

>                    FRIENDLY
>            We've got Annie Lee Moss... We can
>            have that together by next week if
>            need be...

>                    MURROW
>            Is that a whole show?

                                                (CONTINUED)

CONTINUED: (2)

> FRIENDLY
> It's close... Listen Ed, there's
> not going to be a shortage of
> material on him, what we have to
> do now is keep up the pressure
> till his rebuttal... and then move
> to Calcutta...

They smile a long beat.

> MURROW
> Radio... I sure do miss radio.

> FRIENDLY
> You've got a face for radio...

> MURROW
> That's what my wife keeps telling
> me.

Joe and Shirley come back in with several papers stacked
in their arms.

> SHIRLEY
> Alright, here we go... The
> Times...

> SCOTT
> Who wrote it?

> SHIRLEY                          WERSHBA
> Jack Gould.            Gould.

> SHIRLEY
> "Edward R. Murrow's television
> program on Senator Joseph R.
> McCarthy was an exciting and
> provocative examination of the man
> and his methods.  It was crusading
> journalism of high responsibility
> and courage.  For TV so often
> plagued by timidity and
> hesitation, the program was a
> milestone that reflected
> enlightened citizenship."

They all cheer.

> FRIENDLY
> He didn't like it.

> MURROW
> Yeah, what's this guy's beef?

(CONTINUED)

CONTINUED: (3)

                    SHIRLEY
        Hold on... "The program was no
        less an indictment of those who
        wish the problems posed by the
        senator's tactics and theatrics
        would just go away and leave them
        alone.  That was Mr. Murrow's and
        television's triumph, and a very
        great one."

They all cheer.

                    MURROW
        Fritz, send the New York Times a
        bottle of scotch.

                    FRIENDLY
        I already did... how do you think
        we got that review?

                    ZOUSMER
        What about the Post?

                    WERSHBA
        It's pretty good.

                    FRIENDLY
        What about O'Brian?

                    SHIRLEY
        The same.

They all laugh.

                    HOLLENBECK
        Shirley, what'd O'Brian say?

                    SHIRLEY
        I don't have it... Joe, what about
        you?

                    WERSHBA
        It's somewhere here...

He looks through the papers until he finds it, and hands
it to Shirley.

                    SHIRLEY
        Hang on... OK, Jack O'Brian...

Shirley reads from the paper.

                                              (CONTINUED)

31   CONTINUED: (4)                                        31

                         SHIRLEY
          "We can't say we were surprised at
          Edward R. Murrow's 'Hate McCarthy'
          telecast last evening. When his
          explosively one sided propaganda
          edited with deviously clever
          selectivity from McCarthy's March
          against Communism was finished
          last evening, by equally
          Machiavellian coincidence the
          following telecast featured
          Murrow's 'PM' protege Hollenbeck.
          In an obviously gloating mood,
          Hollenbeck hoped viewers had
          witnessed his patrons triumph from
          and for the left."

The room is getting quieter, the mood much less jubilant.
Everyone is aware of the Hollenbeck attacks.

          SHIRLEY                         WERSHBA
...and so on and so on...      I guess O'Brian doesn't
                               like scotch...

                    HOLLENBECK
          It's OK, Shirley... finish it.

          SHIRLEY                         FRIENDLY
That's it... it's just...      Shirley, read the Post...

               HOLLENBECK (CONT'D)
          Finish it, Shirley...

          SHIRLEY                         WERSHBA
That's it, Don.                Yeah, that's it.

Don stares at her until she gives in.

                         SHIRLEY
          Ah... OK, it says "The Columbia
          Broadcasting System has been in a
          lengthy 'clean house of lefties'
          mood. The worst offenders on
          lesser levels have been quietly
          pushed out of the company... Don
          Hollenbeck, a graduate of the
          demised pinko publication 'PM'
          attacked conservative newspapers
          with sly and slanted propaganda...
          he then proceeded through an
          equally tilted review of the day's
          events with McCarthy dominating
          his words, actions, attitude and
          camera..." it's O'Brian.

                                        (CONTINUED)

31     CONTINUED: (5)                                          31

                              SCOTT
                   Is that grammatically correct?

                            HOLLENBECK
                   I'll have that cigarette, Ed.

                                                    CUT TO:

Over black we read, **"That's the Evil of it"**


32     INT. ELEVATOR - CBS - DAY                               32

We start inside an elevator as the doors open on the
second floor, we see Fred walking in. A couple of people
congratulate him on the show. Jimmy's on the elevator.
Going up.

                             FRIENDLY
                   Hey, Jimmy...

                              JIMMY
                   Fred... congratulations...

          FRIENDLY                        JIMMY
     Thanks... it gave me an         All the ad guys watched it
     ulcer....                       on the 3rd floor...

          FRIENDLY                        JIMMY
     Times gave us a great          The switchboard lit up all
     review... Jack Gould...        night. We're gonna put out
     really 15 to 1..               a press release that says
                                    the calls were 15 to 1 in
                                    favor of the show... calls
     Just the east coast, or did    came in from everywhere...
     you hear from...               Kansas City...
                                    Cincinnati...

The door opens on the 10th floor. We see Paley get on
the elevator. The atmosphere changes immediately.
Paley's not in as excited a mood.

          FRIENDLY                        PALEY
     Mr. Paley...                    Good morning... morning,
                                     Fred.

                              JIMMY
                   Good morning, Mr. Paley.

                              PALEY
                   How's your wife, Fred?


                                              (CONTINUED)

32    CONTINUED:                                                      32

                              FRIENDLY
                    She's fine, sir.  We're getting
                    ready to move...

                              PALEY
                    Really?  Where to?

                              FRIENDLY
                    Riverdale.  We found a nice house.

                              PALEY
                    It's nice there.

They ride in silence.  We arrive at the 34th floor.  The
door opens.

                              FRIENDLY
                    Excuse me.

Fred starts to exit.

                              PALEY
                    Fred...

Fred stops and holds the elevator door.

                              PALEY (CONT'D)
                    McCarthy wants William Buckley to
                    do his rebuttal.

                              FRIENDLY
                    Yes, sir.

Fred exits.


33    INT. BULLPEN - DAY                                              33

This scene will be improvised.  All the boys are here.
There is an open discussion going on about Buckley.
Someone reads telegrams out loud, some are discussing who
should pay for the rebuttal and that the response was
fifteen to one in favor of Murrow.

As we still hear what's going on in the bullpen we cut to
Zousmer who is hurrying  down a hallway towards the
bullpen, in his hand he has teletype printout.  Along the
way he pops his head into the copy-room where a few
people are working.

                              ZOUSMER
                    Radulovich has been reinstated.

He then runs into the bullpen amid all the chaos.

                                              (CONTINUED)

33    CONTINUED:                                          33

                              ZOUSMER (CONT'D)
                    Fellas!!  Listen
                    up...fellas...fellas.

He reads from the telegram.

                              ZOUSMER (CONT'D)
                    This is a special announcement
                    from the Secretary of the Air
                    force, Harold E. Talbott.
                    Talbott:  I have decided that it
                    is consistent with the interests
                    of the National Security to retain
                    Lt. Radulovich in the United
                    States Air Force.  He is not in my
                    opinion a security risk.

The room breaks into applause.


34    INT. PROJECTION ROOM                                34

In the darkened room, projected on the screen, is Annie
Lee Moss being questioned by Roy Cohn and McCarthy.

In the foreground silhouetted are MURROW and SCOTT, the
usual.  They will start talking midway through the scene.

                              COHN
                    The committee has had testimony,
                    to which I know you and your
                    counsel are familiar, to the
                    effect that you were at that time
                    a member of the Northeast Club of
                    the Communist Party.  Now is that
                    testimony true?

                              ANNIE LEE MOSS
                    No sir, it is not.  Not at any
                    time have I been a member of a
                    communist party and I have never
                    seen the communist card.

                              COHN
                    You've never seen a communist
                    card?

                              ANNIE LEE MOSS
                    That's right.

                              COHN
                    Have you ever attended any
                    communist meetings?

                                            (CONTINUED)

> ANNIE LEE MOSS
> No, sir.  I've never attended any
> communist meetings.

> COHN
> Have you ever subscribed to "The
> Daily Worker?"

> ANNIE LEE MOSS
> No, sir.  I...didn't...I didn't
> subscribe to "The Daily Worker"
> and I wouldn't pay for it.

> MCCARTHY
> You say that you never have been a
> member of the communist party?

> ANNIE LEE MOSS
> No, sir.  I have not.

> MCCARTHY
> Now, Mrs. Markward, who was
> working for the FBI, joined the
> communist party under orders from
> the FBI has testified that while
> she never met you personally at a
> communist meeting that your name
> was on the list of communists who
> were paying dues.  Can you shed
> any light upon that?

> ANNIE LEE MOSS
> No sir, I...I don't even know what
> the dues are or where they would
> be.

> MCCARTHY
> So I understand, you have never
> paid any money to the communist
> party.  Is that correct?

> ANNIE LEE MOSS
> That's right.

> MCCARTHY
> And you've never attended any
> communist meetings?

> ANNIE LEE MOSS
> No, sir.  I have not.

> MCCARTHY
> Mr. Cohn...

(CONTINUED)

34      CONTINUED: (2)                                         34

                              WERSHBA
                  The sound falls apart.  Charlie
                  pulled the camera back and I
                  couldn't get a mike in close.

          FRIENDLY                              MURROW
    Where does this go...              You can still hear it.
    Ed...                             ... at the end...

    This will continue as an improvised scene about the lead
    up to the Annie Lee Moss story on "See it Now."

    The sound stops as Natalie pops her head in.

    They all look back.

                              NATALIE
                  McCarthy wants April 6th...

    This sits very heavy in the room.

                              FRIENDLY
                  Thanks, Natalie.

    She exits.

                              FRIENDLY (CONT'D)
                  Alright. We go with the Annie Lee
                  Moss story next week.  We'll keep
                  the heat on him... see what he
                  does.

          SCOTT                              WERSHBA
    He'll deny the allegations        Do they want Charlie to
    and go after Stevenson.           shoot it or are they going
                                      to do it?

          FRIENDLY                            WERSHBA
    What allegations?  He's not       It'd be nice if they just
    going to deny his own words       let Charlie shoot it.  We'd
    on film...we used his             get to see it first.
    words.

                              MURROW
                  We know what it'll be.

    They all listen.

                              MURROW (CONT'D)
                  He's gonna come after me.  It's
                  the only thing he can do.  He's
                  going to bet that a Senator trumps
                  a Newsman.

                                                    (CONTINUED)

34        CONTINUED: (3)                                    34

                            FRIENDLY
                  He'll lose.

                            MURROW
                  Maybe.

         DON HOLLENBECK sticks his head in.

                            HOLLENBECK
                  Ed.  You got a minute?

                            MURROW
                  Yeah, Don.

                            FRIENDLY
                  Okay, fellas.  Annie Lee Moss.
                  Joe, call legal let'em know.

              WERSHBA                        FRIENDLY
         This will be fun.           Eddie, let's see all the
                                     Moss footage you've cut.

         MURROW & HOLLENBECK exit.

                                                  CUT TO:


35        INT. COPYING ROOM - DAY                           35


              MURROW                        HOLLENBECK
         Sit down.  I missed you the   I need to ask you
         other night, I'm sorry I      something... Ed...
         was...
                                       it's about O'Brian...
         O'Brian doesn't matter...
                                       He's killing me... he...
         O'Brian doesn't amount to a   Ed...
         hell of a lot in a newsroom
         Don.

                            HOLLENBECK
                  It's not just him... we have to
                  let this guy have it, he's... we
                  should expose O'Brian for the--

                            MURROW
                  We're not going after O'Brian,
                  Don.  I won't take on McCarthy and
                  Hearst.  I can't beat them both.
                  Don't read the papers... or...
                  don't read O'Brian anyway.


                                             (CONTINUED)

Beat.

                    HOLLENBECK
          No, I guess not.

There is a long pause.

                    HOLLENBECK (CONT'D)
          I wake up in the morning, and I
          don't recognize anything.  I feel
          like I went to sleep three years
          ago and somebody hijacked... as if
          all reasonable people took a plane
          to Europe and left us behind...
          trying to make sense out of...
          insanity... I was always an
          optimist... really... I always
          felt like things would work out...
          half full...

                    MURROW
          I believe that... it's the beauty
          of all this... we designed it so
          we can fix it... Jefferson built
          it into the Constitution...

                    HOLLENBECK
          I was talking about my divorce...

They smile.

                    MURROW
          So was I...

A sad smile.

                    HOLLENBECK
          Well, I'm glad the Forefathers
          understood the term "Dissolution
          of a Union..."

                    MURROW
          I'm sure they had their share of
          difficulties with the opposite
          sex.

                    HOLLENBECK
          I'm talking about McCarthy.

They smile again.

                    MURROW
          So am I.

(CONTINUED)

35    CONTINUED: (2)                                        35

A sad grin.

                    HOLLENBECK
          Okay.  I thought I'd try.

                    MURROW
          Sorry, Don.

Hollenbeck starts to leave, he stops and turns to Murrow.

                    HOLLENBECK
          We didn't have this
          conversation... okay?

Murrow talks too loudly into the ceiling lamp.

                    MURROW
          IF IT'S OKAY WITH YOU, SENATOR!

                    HOLLENBECK
                (As he exits)
          Don't laugh... I've thought
          about it.

36    NOTE: THIS NEXT SCENE WILL START IN A RECORDING BOOTH   36
      AS MURROW RECORDS HIS VOICEOVER FOR THE ANNIE LEE MOSS
      FOOTAGE. WE SEE THE FOOTAGE ON THE STUDIO MONITOR. WE MAY
      HEAR SOME OF THIS. WE'LL SHOOT THROUGH DOORWAYS AND BACKS
      OF ROOMS ALL THE WHILE MRS. MOSS WILL BE TESTIFYING....

McCarthy questions Annie Lee Moss.

                    MCCARTHY
          I'm afraid I'm going to have to
          excuse myself.  I've got a rather
          important appointment to make
          which I've got to work on right
          now...Senator Mundt, if you could
          take over as chairman.

                    SYMINGTON
          May I suggest that she be asked
          how many times she saw Robert
          Hall?

                    COHN
          About how many times...

                    MURROW (V.O.)
          That was Senator Symington of
          Missouri.

                                           (CONTINUED)

                         ANNIE LEE MOSS
              Well, each time I went to the
              union...

                         MURROW (V.O.)
              Senator Mundt.  South Dakota.

                         COHN
              Mrs. Moss testified in Executive
              session that Robert Hall...

                         MURROW (V.O.)
              Mr. Cohn wanted to know about Mrs.
              Moss' connection with Rob Hall, an
              alleged communist leader in
              Washington.  But this Rob Hall was
              known to be a white man.

                         COHN
              We can assume that is the same Rob
              Hall...

                         SYMINGTON
              Maybe we could check.

                         COHN
              If there is another one or
              anything like that, we'll
              certainly explore...

                         SYMINGTON
              Let's...let's get to that...is the
              Robert Hall you know a colored
              man?

                         ANNIE LEE MOSS
              Yes, sir.

                         SYMINGTON
              You're sure of that?

                         ANNIE LEE MOSS
              Yes, I think...I'm pretty sure
              he's colored.

                         SYMINGTON
              Does he look like a colored man or
              does he look more like a white
              man?

                         ANNIE LEE MOSS
              The man who I have in mind as
              Robert Hall is a man about my
              complexion.

                                           (CONTINUED)

36    CONTINUED: (2)                                          36

                              SYMINGTON
                    About your complexion?

                              ANNIE LEE MOSS
                    Yes.

                              SYMINGTON
                    So it's fair to say you didn't
                    think that he was a white man?

                              ANNIE LEE MOSS
                    No, sir.  I didn't.

                              SYMINGTON
                    I'd like to put in the record that
                    one of the reporters said that he
                    is certain that Robert Hall of
                    "The Daily Worker" is a white man.

                                              CUT TO:

37    INT. CONTROL ROOM - NIGHT                               37

The "See It Now" show is in progress, Murrow is in his
chair on the set.  We see the now famous exchange between
Roy Cohn and Senator McClellan.

                              SENATOR SYMINGTON
                    Have you ever had any information
                    that you received in your job that
                    you passed on to anybody about
                    these codes?

                              ANNIE LEE MOSS
                    No, sir.

                              SENATOR SYMINGTON
                    Did anybody ever ask you to, for
                    any of that information?

                              ANNIE LEE MOSS
                    No, sir.  If they had, I would
                    have reported 'em.

                              SENATOR SYMINGTON
                    You would have reported them?

                              ANNIE LEE MOSS
                    I certainly would have.

                              SENATOR SYMINGTON
                    Has anyone ever asked you to join
                    the Communist party?

                                           (CONTINUED)

37    CONTINUED:                                                    37

> ANNIE LEE MOSS
> No, sir.
>
> SENATOR SYMINGTON
> Has anybody ever asked you to join
> any organization of any kind that
> you thought might be against the
> best interest of the United
> States?
>
> ANNIE LEE MOSS
> No, sir.
>
> SENATOR SYMINGTON
> What are you living on now?  Have
> you got any savings?
>
> ANNIE LEE MOSS
> No, sir.
>
> SENATOR SYMINGTON
> You haven't?
>
> ANNIE LEE MOSS
> No, sir.
>
> SENATOR SYMINGTON
> If you, uh, uh, uh, don't get
> work, uh, pretty soon, what are
> you going to do?
>
> ANNIE LEE MOSS
> Going down to welfare.
>
> SENATOR SYMINGTON
> Going down to welfare.
>
> ANNIE LEE MOSS
> Uh-huh.
>
> ROY COHN
> I have no further questions of
> this witness at this time.  I can
> say this, we have the testimony of
> Miss Markward, the undercover
> agent for the FBI, stating that
> Annie Lee was, was a member, a
> dues-paying member of the
> Communist Party, uh... the
> Northeast Club of the Communist
> Party.
> (MORE)

(CONTINUED)

37        CONTINUED: (2)

                    ROY COHN (CONT'D)
          We have corroboration of that
          testimony by another witness who
          was called before the committee
          and gave their sworn statement to
          the effect that she also knew Mrs.
          Moss as a member of the Northeast
          Club of the Communist Party.

                    SENATOR MCCLELLAN
          Well, Mr. Chairman, I'd like to
          make... we're making a statement
          here against a witness who has
          come and submitted to cross-
          examination. Now, she's already
          lost her job. She's been
          suspended because of this action.
          I'm not defending her. If she's a
          Communist, I want her exposed.
          But, to make these statements as
          we've corroborating evidence that
          she is a Communist. Under these
          circumstances, I think she's
          entitled to have it produced here
          in her presence and let the public
          know about it and let her know
          about it.

There is applause.

                    SENATOR MCCLELLAN (CONT'D)
          I don't like to try people by
          hearsay evidence.

More applause.


38        EXT. TV REPAIR SHOP                        38

We are now out on the street, looking at televisions
through the window.

                    SENATOR MCCLELLAN
          I'd like to get the witnesses here
          and try 'em-- by testimony, under
          oath.

                    CHAIRMAN MUNDT
          The, uh, chair will rule that the
          comment of Mr. Cohn be stricken
          from the record.

                    SENATOR MCCLELLAN
          Well, I didn't ask that. I didn't
          ask that, Mr. Chairman.

39      INT. PENTAGON BAR      39

Patrons watch the television...

> CHAIRMAN MUNDT
> ... executive session whether we
> should try to, uh, produce a
> witness in public because the FBI
> may have her undercover and we
> don't want to, uh-

> SENATOR MCCLELLAN
> You can't strike these statements
> made by counsel here as to
> evidence that we're having and
> withholding. You cannot strike
> that from the press nor from the
> public mind once it's planted
> there. That's the, that is the,
> uh, the evil of it. And I don't
> think it's fair to a witness, to a
> citizen of this country, to bring
> 'em up here and cross-examine 'em.
> Then when they get through say,
> "We've got something, the FBI has
> got something on you that condemns
> you." It is not sworn testimony,
> it's convicting people by rumor
> and hearsay and innuendo.

Applause.

CUT TO:

40      INT. "SEE IT NOW" STAGE      40

We're watching MURROW as he closes the show.

> MURROW
> You will notice that neither
> Senator McClellan or Senator
> Symington nor this reporter know
> or claim that Mrs. Moss was or is
> a communist. Their claim was
> simply, that she had the right to
> meet her accusers face to face.

CUT TO:

A card that reads, **April, 6 1954**

41          INT. CONTROL ROOM - SHOW NIGHT                    41

This scene will be built with a lot of very tight close
ups of crew and reporters.  Everyone is very aware of
their vulnerability.  Cameramen glancing at one another.
Stage Manager focusing on the monitor.

Right now it's silent as they wait for MURROW to arrive.

We pull Ed in a close up as he enters into the room and
sees the film canisters.

                    HEWITT
          Ed, it's twenty eight minutes.  I
          could clip a little off the end
          for you to have time to...

                    MURROW
          I think we have to leave it alone,
          Don.

He starts tearing out pages.

                    MURROW (CONT'D)
          Very smart, no time for comment...
          when did it come in?

                    HEWITT
          Ten minutes ago.  We put it up, I
          saw the first couple of minutes,
          you're right.

                    MURROW
          Coming after me?

HEWITT nods.

                    MURROW (CONT'D)
          Joe, have you seen the latest
          polls?... The most trustworthy man
          in America is Milton Berle.

                    WERSHBA
          Maybe he should do the story.

                    MURROW
          Get him on the line, will ya?

MURROW walks onto the stage.  FRIENDLY'S there.  Against
the back wall are Murrow's team.

                    MURROW (CONT'D)
          Fred.

                                        (CONTINUED)

> FRIENDLY
> What say we grab a little dinner
> after the show?  The 21 Club?

> MURROW
> Sure.

He sits noticing The Boys.  They give little waves,
MURROW acknowledges them.

> MURROW (CONT'D)
> What're they here for?  "The
> Monkey and the Bell" show is on
> stage three.

> FRIENDLY
> They changed the title.  "Goin'
> Ape."

> MURROW
> Who's their first guest?

The loudspeaker - "Thirty seconds to Air"

> FRIENDLY
> After tonight, I hear it's you.

They smile.

> FRIENDLY (CONT'D)
> Look, there's nothing fun about
> this one.  You've just gotta put
> your gloves down, stick your chin
> out and just take it for a whole
> round.  Next week's our round.

> MURROW
> If I make it up off the mat.

MURROW takes out a cigarette, FRIENDLY lights it.

Loudspeaker - "Twenty seconds to air"

> FRIENDLY
> You will.

> MURROW
> Did you see the latest polls,
> Milton Berle's the most trusted
> man in America...

> FRIENDLY
> You already did this joke for
> me...

(CONTINUED)

They look at each other.

>                    FRIENDLY (CONT'D)
>          I'll get Berle on the line.

Loudspeaker - "Ten seconds"

MURROW sits there again in silence.  The weight of the
world sitting there with him.

>                    STAGE MANAGER
>          In five, four, three, two...

He points to MURROW.

We come up on the monitor as MURROW speaks directly at
us.

>                    MURROW
>          One month ago tonight we presented
>          a report on Senator Joseph R.
>          McCarthy.  We labeled it as
>          controversial.  Most of that
>          report consisted of words and
>          pictures of the Senator.  At that
>          time, we said if the Senator
>          believes we have done violence to
>          his words or pictures, if he
>          desires to speak, to answer
>          himself, an opportunity would be
>          afforded him on this program.  The
>          Senator sought the opportunity,
>          asked for a delay of three weeks
>          because he said he was very busy
>          and he wished adequate time to
>          prepare his reply.  We agreed.  We
>          placed no restrictions on the
>          manner or method of the
>          presentation of his reply and we
>          suggested that we would not take
>          time to comment on this program.
>          Here now is Senator Joseph R.
>          McCarthy, Junior Senator from
>          Wisconsin.

McCarthy begins.  As he delivers his rebuttal we will cut
to various places that it is airing.

For the moment we're right on MURROW as he watches.

                                              (CONTINUED)

41        CONTINUED: (3)                                    41

                              MCCARTHY
                    Good evening.  Mr. Edward R.
                    Murrow, Educational Director of
                    the Columbia Broadcasting System,
                    devoted his program to an attack
                    on the work of the United States
                    Senate investigating committee and
                    on me personally as its Chairman.
                    Now, over the past four years, he
                    has made repeated attacks upon me
                    and those fighting communists.
                    Now, of course, neither Joe
                    McCarthy nor Edward R. Murrow is
                    of any great importance as
                    individuals.  We are only
                    important in our relations to the
                    great struggle to preserve our
                    American liberties.

                                                        CUT TO:


42        INT. PALEY'S OFFICE                             42

          PALEY watches in silence.
                    Now ordinarily, I wouldn't take
                    time out of the important work at
                    hand to answer Murrow.  However in
                    this case I felt justified in
                    doing so because Murrow is a
                    symbol, the leader and the
                    cleverest of the jackal pack which
                    is always found at the throat of
                    anyone who dares expose individual
                    communists and traitors.

                                                        CUT TO:


43        INT. JOE & SHIRLEY WERSHBA'S NY APT.            43

          Shirley watches.
                    I am compelled by the fact to say
                    to you that Mr. Edward R. Murrow,
                    as far back as twenty years ago
                    was engaged in propaganda for
                    communist causes.  For example,
                    the Institute for International
                    Education of which he was the
                    Acting Director, was chosen to act
                    as a representative by a Soviet
                    agency to do a job which would
                    normally be done by the Russian
                    Secret Police.

                                                    (CONTINUED)

43     CONTINUED:                                          43

Back to MURROW on the set.
          Mr. Murrow sponsored a communist
          school in Moscow...

This speech will continue but we'll hear MURROW and
FRIENDLY talking.

                    MURROW
          When the politicians complain that
          TV turns the proceedings into a
          circus, it should be clear that
          the circus was already there, and
          that TV has only demonstrated that
          not all the performers are well
          trained.

                    FRIENDLY
          We've got him, Ed.

                    MURROW
          If he led with his best.

                    FRIENDLY
          He led with his best.

                                          CUT TO:


44     INT. PALEY'S OFFICE                                 44

                    MCCARTHY
          Now, Mr. Murrow, by his own
          admission, was a member of the
          IWW, that's the Industrial Workers
          of the World, a terrorist
          organization cited by an Attorney
          General of the United States...

                                          CUT TO:


45     INT. HALLWAY CBS                                    45

It's empty.  McCarthy's voice echoing.

                    MCCARTHY
          Now, Mr. Murrow said on this
          program and I quote, he said, "The
          actions of the Junior Senator from
          Wisconsin have given considerable
          comfort to the enemy."

MURROW walks into the hall followed by FRIENDLY, WERSHBA,
MACK, they walk toward us as the speech continues.

                                          (CONTINUED)

45    CONTINUED:                                        45

                              MCCARTHY (CONT'D)
                  That is the language of our
                  statute of treason.  If I am
                  giving comfort to our enemies, I
                  ought not to be in the Senate.  If
                  on the other hand, Mr. Murrow is
                  giving comfort to the enemies, he
                  ought not to be brought into the
                  homes of Americans by the Columbia
                  Broadcasting System.

As they exit we stay on the empty hallway.

We fade to black as McCarthy drones on.


46    WE'LL PLAY AN ALCOA COMMERCIAL HERE               46


47    INT. "SEE IT NOW" SET                             47

We are on the set of "See it Now" as MURROW addresses us
directly.

                              MURROW
                  Last week, Senator McCarthy
                  appeared on this program to
                  correct any errors he might have
                  thought we made in our report of
                  March 9th.  Since he made no
                  reference to any statements of
                  fact that we made, we must
                  conclude that he found no errors
                  of fact.  He proved again that
                  anyone who exposes him, anyone who
                  does not share his hysterical
                  disregard to decency and human
                  dignity and the rights guaranteed
                  by the Constitution must be either
                  a Communist or a fellow traveler.
                  I fully expected this treatment.
                  The Senator added this reporter's
                  name to a long list of individuals
                  and institutions he has accused of
                  serving the communist cause.  His
                  proposition is very simple:
                  Anyone who criticizes or opposes
                  McCarthy's methods must be a
                  Communist.  And if that be true,
                  there are an awful lot of
                  Communists in this country.  For
                  the record, let's consider briefly
                  some of the Senator's charges.
                              (MORE)

                                          (CONTINUED)

47  CONTINUED:            47

          MURROW (CONT'D)
       He claimed but offered no proof
       that I had been a member of the
       Industrial Workers of the World.
       That is false.  I was never a
       member of the IWW, never applied
       for membership.

                CUT TO:


48  INT. CONTROL BOOTH          48

We cut to the control booth, PALMER WILLIAMS and company
watch on as the broadcast continues.

         WILLIAMS
       Ready two... hold it...hold...
       take two... tell 'em Ed.

         MURROW
       The Senator charged that Professor
       Harold Laski, a British scholar
       and politician dedicated a book to
       me.  That's true.  He is dead.  He
       was a Socialist, I am not.  He was
       one of those civilized individuals
       who did not insist upon agreement
       with his political principles as a
       pre-condition for conversation or
       friendship.  I do not agree with
       his political ideas.  Laski, as he
       makes clear in the introduction,
       dedicated the book to me not
       because of political agreement but
       because he held my wartime
       broadcast from London in high
       regard; and the dedication so
       reads.

         WILLIAMS
       Ready on one... closer, Charlie...
       take one...

                CUT TO:


49  INT. "SEE IT NOW" SET         49

Again MURROW addresses us directly.


               (CONTINUED)

49      CONTINUED:                                                      49

                            MURROW
            I believed twenty years ago and I
            believe today that mature
            Americans can engage in
            conversation and controversy, the
            clash of ideas, with Communists
            anywhere in the world without
            becoming contaminated or
            converted.  I believe that our
            faith, our conviction, our
            determination are stronger than
            theirs and that we can compete and
            successfully, not only in the area
            of bombs but in the area of ideas.

                                                        CUT TO:


50      INT. PALEY'S OFFICE                                             50

        As PALEY watches on a television.
            I have worked for CBS for more
            than nineteen years.  The company
            has subscribed fully to my
            integrity and responsibility as a
            broadcaster and as a loyal
            American.  I require no lectures
            from the junior Senator from
            Wisconsin as to the dangers or
            terrors of Communism - having
            watched the aggressive forces at
            work in Western Europe.

                                                        CUT TO:


51      INT. "SEE IT NOW" SET                                           51
            Having had friends in Eastern
            Europe butchered and driven in
            exile, having broadcast from
            London in 1943 that the Russians
            were responsible for the Katyn
            Massacre - having told the story
            of the Russian refusal to allow
            allied aircraft to land on Russian
            fields after dropping supplies to
            those who rose in Warsaw and then
            were betrayed by the Russians.

                                                        CUT TO:

52      INT. BULLPEN                                          52

Murrow's team watch and smoke.

                        WERSHBA
                       (Quietly)
             Go Ed.

                        MURROW
             And having been denounced by the
             Russian radio for these reports.
             I cannot feel that I require
             instruction from the Senator on
             the evils of Communism.

                                              CUT TO:


53      INT. "SEE IT NOW" SET                                 53

MURROW addresses us directly.
             Having searched my conscience and
             my files, I cannot contend that I
             have always been right or wise
             but, I have attempted to pursue
             the truth with some diligence and
             to report it, even though as in
             this case I had been warned in
             advance that I would be subjected
             to the attentions of Senator
             McCarthy.  We shall hope to deal
             with matters of more vital
             interest to the country next week.
             Good night.  And, good luck.

We go to a commercial.  As we hear it play, we see Murrow
stand up.  He shakes people's hands, there are some pats
on the back... not victorious... not afraid... simply a
job well done.

Murrow looks over to Friendly who lights Murrow's
cigarette.

                        MURROW
             That ought to hold him.

                        FRIENDLY
             Are you a gambling man?

                        MURROW
             Just with your career.


                                              (CONTINUED)

53      CONTINUED:                                                    53

                              FRIENDLY
                             (smiles)
                    Not just mine...

He nods in the direction of Wershba, Zousmer, Aaron and
Scott, smoking in the back of the stage.

Murrow waves to his boys and they wave back.

We hear the song "How High The Moon" under this shot.

                                                    CUT TO:

54      INT. SOUNDSTAGE - SHOWER OF STARS                           54

A singer rehearses "How High the Moon" with her band.  We
track back from the soundstage into the Hallway onto John
Aarons.  Under the music and the shot of Aarons we hear
Murrow, Friendly, Zousmer, Scott and Williams.  Zousmer
reads from a newspaper.

                         ZOUSMER (V.O.)
                    "In the last analysis, the Senator
                    was perched on the television high
                    dive and all prepared to make a
                    resounding splash.  He jumped
                    beautifully, but neglected to
                    check first where he was going to
                    land.  It must have been something
                    of a shock to discover that Mr.
                    Murrow had drained the water out
                    of the pool."

            ZOUSMER (V.O.)                  MURROW (V.O.)
    Jack Gould... yeah, the          Jesus.  Is that the Times?
    Times.                           Gould?

                         MURROW  (V.O.)
                    He's a hell of a writer, I'll tell
                    you that.  You should hire him
                    away from the Times...

                         SCOTT (V.O.)
                    Well, Stanton's got a public
                    opinion survey that Elmo Roper put
                    together that says that 33% of
                    households believe McCarthy proved
                    you're a commie...

                         MURROW (V.O.)
                    Only 33%?

JOHN AARON enters.

                                                    (CONTINUED)

54      CONTINUED:                                                    54

                              AARON
                    The Senate's investigating
                    McCarthy.

This is a great moment for Murrow and his boys. As they
celebrate the phone rings. Friendly picks it up but we
can't hear what he says. He puts the phone down and
walks over to Murrow.

                              FRIENDLY
                    Listen, Ed...

                              MURROW
                    We're a hit... up there with Howdy
                    Doody.

                              FRIENDLY
                    Hold on Ed.

The two men look at each other. Fred says something to
Murrow that we can't hear. A look of disbelief spreads
across Murrow's face. This sits with the two men as
Murrow gets up and walks through the hall and into the
control room, where he sits alone.

Our singer continues to sing which will score the rest of
the scene. Over these scenes we will also hear the voice
of Joe Wershba.

                              WERSHBA  (V.O.)
                    "Don Hollenbeck was one of the
                    most prominent members of the CBS
                    lefties. And, he hewed to its
                    incipient pink line without
                    deviation."

                                                          CUT TO:


55      INT. DON HOLLENBECK'S APARTMENT                               55

Hollenbeck alone, is taking towels and placing them along
the baseboards of his one room apartment.

                              WERSHBA (V.O.)
                    "He was a reactionary leftist. He
                    drew assignments which paid him
                    lush fees, pink painting his news
                    items and analysis always with a
                    steady left hand."

                                                          CUT TO:

56      INT. CONTROL ROOM      56

We see a close up of Murrow as he sits smoking. Behind him we see the news spreading rapidly through the boys.

>             WERSHBA (V.O.)
>"Hollenbeck was a graduate of
>several suspicious training posts.
>He was with the Office Of War
>Information when it was loaded
>with commies."

                                   CUT TO:


57      INT. BULLPEN      57

Friendly just sits there re-reading the note, everyone else stares silently.

>             WERSHBA (V.O.)
>"He did a stretch as a top editor
>of the commie-laden newspaper PM,
>whose staff was infiltrated slyly
>by a slew of sinister types not
>equalled this side of the daily
>worker."

                                   CUT TO:


58      INT. DON HOLLENBECK'S APARTMENT      58

We see Hollenbeck turn up the gas on his oven but not light it. He leaves the oven door open and sits back in his chair to wait for his long needed sleep.

>             WERSHBA (V.O.)
>"The fact of Newscaster Don
>Hollenbeck's suicide yesterday
>does not remove from the record
>the peculiar history of the
>leftist slanting of news indulged
>consistently by the Columbia
>Broadcasting System."

Our SINGER stops the band and finishes the song accapella.

                                   CUT TO:

59      INT. BULLPEN                                            59

Friendly sits silently.

                                                        CUT TO:

60      INT. CONTROL ROOM                                       60

Murrow sits, his back leaning against the wall.

                                                        CUT TO:

61      INT. DON HOLLENBECK'S APARTMENT                         61

TV light flickers a test pattern and the familiar high
pitched tone of a network that has signed off for the
evening.

Slumped in his chair in the shadows, is Hollenbeck.

"How High the Moon" ends.

                                                        CUT TO:

62      INT. BULLPEN                                            62

Williams, Scott and Mack sit silently as Joe Wershba
finishes reading aloud from a newspaper.

                        WERSHBA (V.O.)
                "Hollenbeck was what most astute
                students of CBS's strange and
                questionable new methods
                considered 'typical of its
                newscasters'"...

Beat.

                        WERSHBA (V.O.) (CONT'D)
                ... by Jack O'Brian.

They sit in silence.

                        SCOTT
                        (Quietly)
                What time is it?

                        MACK
                Nine-forty.

                                                    (CONTINUED)

                        SCOTT
He wrote that... not twelve hours
after Don was dead...

Beat.

                  SCOTT (CONT'D)
The son of a bitch.

                       MACK
Let's see what we can find on Jack
O'Brian.

They sit there.

                    WERSHBA
And then, what are we?... Don
Hollenbeck had a troubled
marriage... and he died... he had
the decency not to leave a note.

More silence.

                WERSHBA (CONT'D)
... And because of that no one
will ever remember Jack O'Brian.

Wershba exits. We pan over to include the bullpen
monitor and see Murrow give a last minute obituary. We
watch it with the boys.

                    MURROW
One of the best programs I ever
heard was called "CBS Views The
Press." A great many people liked
it, some didn't, but no one ever
said it was anything but honest.
It was the work of an honest
reporter. Don Hollenbeck. He
also worked occasionally on "See
It Now." He did the 11 PM News
over some of these stations.

He had been sick lately and he
died this morning. The police
said it was suicide. Gas.

Not much of an Obit... but, at
least we got our facts straight...
and it was brief. And, that's all
Don Hollenbeck would have asked.

Good night. And, good luck.

(CONTINUED)

62    CONTINUED: (2)                                        62

Over black we read:  **"At long last have you no sense of decency?"**

63    OMITTED                                               63

64    INT. JOE & SHIRLEY WERSHBA'S NY APT. - NIGHT          64

Joe and Shirley sit on the couch watching TV.  On the screen we see McCarthy being questioned by the Army's Special Counsel Joseph Welch.

                    WELSH
          Did you realize when you took that
          oath that you were making a solemn
          promise to tell the whole truth to
          this committee?

                    MCCARTHY
          I understand the oath, Mr. Welsh.

                    WELSH
          And when you took it, did you have
          some mental reservations, some
          fifth or sixth amendment notion
          that you could measure what you
          would tell?

                    MCCARTHY
          I don't take the fifth or sixth
          amendment.

                    WELSH
          Have you some private reservation
          when you take the oath that you
          will tell the whole truth; that
          lets you be the judge of what you
          will testify to?

                    MCCARTHY
          The answer is there is no
          reservation about telling the
          whole truth.

                    WELSH
          Thank you, sir.

                                                    CUT TO:

65    INT. JOE & SHIRLEY WERSHBA'S NY APT. - NIGHT          65

Joe and Shirley are in bed.  Neither can sleep, they both stare up at the ceiling.  We sit in silence for a bit.

                                                (CONTINUED)

                         JOE
              What time is it?

                         SHIRLEY
              About two...

                         JOE
              I have to be in Philadelphia this
              morning.

                         SHIRLEY
              What time is your train?

                         JOE
              Eight.

                         SHIRLEY
              Charlie going with you?

                         JOE
              Yes.

A beat of silence.

                         JOE (CONT'D)
              Here's a thought...what if we're
              wrong.

                         SHIRLEY
              About?

                         JOE
              What if we're wrong?

Beat.

                         SHIRLEY
              We're not wrong.

                         JOE
              So we're not going to look back
              and say we protected the wrong
              side...

                         SHIRLEY
              Protected them from what...in the
              name of what?... What would we be
              preserving?

                         JOE
              You could make an argument
              for,"The greater good."

                                          (CONTINUED)

65    CONTINUED: (2)                                          65

                            SHIRLEY
                  Not once you give it all
                  away...it's no good then.

                            JOE
                  It was just a thought...

                                                    CUT TO:


66    INT. PERSON TO PERSON - DAY                             66

We're close on a monitor as we watch McCarthy now being
grilled by the Senate. Everyone is glued to the TV.

We track out of the bullpen and onto the "Person to
Person" set.  The show is close to starting.  MURROW, in
his chair is also watching the hearings on a stage
monitor.

The stage Manager counts down as the sound of the
hearings is turned down.

Five, four, three, two...

Murrow starts his interview with Gina Lollabrigida and
her husband Milko Scofic.

During the interview when the camera is not on him,
Murrow watches the hearings. He only goes through the
motions with Gina and Milko.

                            GINA
                  Hello.

                            MURROW
                  Milko...

                            MILKO
                  Good evening, how are you?

                            MURROW
                  I'm sorry my Italian is so bad.

                            GINA
                  Oh, don't feel so worried.  My
                  English is...is bad too.

                            MURROW
                  Milko, Gina's had quite a week
                  here but, uh, I suppose you're
                  both used to that now aren't you?


                                              (CONTINUED)

66    CONTINUED:                                              66

>                         MILKO
>           Oh yes, quite. New York is always
>           quite harder than any place else
>           because it's such a big city, but
>           we get used to it.
>
>                         MURROW
>           Gina, you met Vice President Nixon
>           on Saturday I believe. Did you
>           two talk any politics at all?
>
>                         GINA
>           Oh no. How, how I can? He was
>           very nice with me. We...he said
>           that he's a movie fan um, of my
>           old Italian films and I was very
>           happy to hear this because we need
>           many, many fans because of the
>           television. Everybody look at the
>           television now. And then we talk
>           about fashion.
>
>                         MURROW
>           About fashion? Uh, what did you
>           two agree on about fashion?
>
>                         GINA
>           Uh, we uh, both don't like this
>           uh, sack line, new sack line. You
>           know I don't want to look like
>           this new, uh, this modern
>           painting. Uh...where the eyes are
>           on the knee and the bosoms back
>           here. I don't want to mean that
>           this new fashion is uh, is not
>           chic. I think it's just not good
>           for me.
>
>                         MURROW
>           Not for you. Uh, Milko, uh,
>           anything you care to say on that
>           subject?
>
>                         MILKO
>           Uh, I think no comment.

As Gina and Milko drone on, we take out the sound and
hear an exchange between Joseph Welch and McCarthy.

>                         MCCARTHY
>           ...And I want to say, Mr. Welch,
>           that it had been labeled long
>           before he became a member. As
>           early as 1944...

                                                    (CONTINUED)

66    CONTINUED: (2)    

                  WELCH
May we not drop this...we know he
belonged to the Lawyer's Guild and
Mr. Cohn nods his head at me.  I
did you, I think, no personal
injury, Mr. Cohn

                  COHN
No, sir.

                  WELCH
I meant to do you no personal
injury.

                  COHN
No.

                  WELCH
And if I did, I beg your pardon.
Let us not assassinate this lad
further, Senator.  You've done
enough.  Have you no sense of
decency, sir?  At long last, have
you left no sense of decency?

                  MCCARTHY
I know this hurts you, Mr. Welch.

                  WELCH
I'll say-

                  MCCARTHY
But may I say, Mr. Chairman, as a
point of personal privilege, I'd
like to finish this.

                  WELCH
Senator, I think it hurts you too
sir.

                  MCCARTHY
I'd like to finish this.

                  WELCH
Mr. McCarthy, I will not discuss
this further with you.  You have
sat within six feet of me.  You
could have asked me about Fred
Fisher.  You have seen fit to
bring it out and if there is a God
in heaven, it will do neither you,
nor your case any good.  I will
not discuss it further.
                  (MORE)

                              (CONTINUED)

66      CONTINUED: (3)                                    66
                          WELCH (CONT'D)
                I will not ask Mr. Cohn any more
                witnesses.  You, Mr. Chairman, may
                if you will, call the next
                witness.

                                                    CUT TO:


67      INT. BULLPEN                                      67

SIG MICKELSON, walks down through the newsroom, he spots
Wershba typing.  Shirley is across the office on the
phone.

                          MICKELSON
                Joe... where's Shirley?

Wershba looks up not sure what's going on.  He points to
Shirley on the phone.

                          MICKELSON (CONT'D)
                Shirley?  Can I talk to you both?

                          WERSHBA
                Okay... let's go into the
                projection room.

                          MICKELSON
                Fine... Shirley... how are you?

As they walk into the announcers booth.

                          SHIRLEY
                Fine, Sig.

                          MICKELSON
                Sit down.

                          WERSHBA
                Is there a problem, Sig?

                          MICKELSON
                You both are aware that there is a
                policy here at CBS that no two
                employees can be married.

JOE and SHIRLEY sit silently.

                          MICKELSON (CONT'D)
                I want to ask you both a question,
                but I don't want you to answer it.
                Just consider it.  I know you two
                are married...

They both just sit there looking straight ahead.

                                                    (CONTINUED)

                              MICKELSON (CONT'D)
Everyone knows... that's not my
question... in the next few weeks
I have to lay a couple of people
off... we're making some
significant cuts across the board.
I wanted you to know that.
Because if you have any intention,
in the near future, of starting a
family, I would say to you, that
you could save someone else from
being fired.  I'm asking you to
consider making this decision a
little easier.  I don't need an
answer now.  Just think about it.

Mickelson stands and leaves.

Joe and Shirley just sit there.

After a few beats they start to slowly quietly laugh.
There is a melancholy to this moment.

Joe reaches into his pocket, pulls out his wedding ring
and places it on his finger, Shirley does the same.

                              WERSHBA
Well, Mrs. Wershba...

                              SHIRLEY
We're going to miss you around
here, Joe.

They stand to leave.

                              WERSHBA
I'll pack my things.

                              SHIRLEY
I think it's for the best.

As they exit.

Finally.

                              WERSHBA
Everybody knew.

                                        CUT TO:

68     INT. CBS EXECUTIVE HALLWAY - NIGHT                       68

We follow MURROW as he walks towards PALEY'S office.

                                       (CONTINUED)

68  CONTINUED:                                          68

Under this we hear in V.O.

                    MURROW (V.O.)
               Natalie... did he say what it's
               about?

                    NATALIE (V.O.)
               No, Mr. Murrow.  Just that he
               wanted to speak to you in his
               office...

                    MURROW (V.O.)
               Have you no sense of decency
               Natalie?

69  INT. PALEY'S WAITING ROOM                           69

Friendly is seated on the couch as Murrow walks in.
Murrow walks over and sits down next to Friendly.

                    MURROW
               Uh Oh.

Fred smiles and the two just sit in silence, then we
hear....

70  INT. PALEY'S OFFICE                                 70

Paley is seated at his desk, across from him sit Murrow
and Friendly.

                    PALEY
               The problem isn't simply that
               you've lost your sponsor.  <u>With</u>
               Alcoa, "See It Now" still loses
               money.

                    FRIENDLY
               The fee is fifty-thousand.  And
               last week's show we did for less
               than the fee.

                    PALEY
               Fred, you're speaking beyond your
               competence.

                                          (CONTINUED)

MURROW
We'll find another
sponsor... we can certainly
find someone who wants
to...

PALEY
"$64,000 Question" brings
in over eighty-thousand in
sponsors and costs a third
of what you do.

PALEY (CONT'D)
Ed. I've got Tuesday night
programming that's number one.
People want to enjoy themselves.
They don't want a civics lesson.

MURROW
Well what do you want Bill?

PALEY
I don't want a constant stomach
ache every time you do a
controversial subject.

MURROW
I'm afraid that's the price you
have to be willing to pay.

PALEY
Careful Ed. Let's walk carefully
through these next few moments...

MURROW
But the content of what we're
doing is more important... than
what some guy in Cincinnati...

PALEY
...What you're doing Ed.  Not me.
Not Frank Stanton.  You.

MURROW
"CBS News," "See It Now" all
belong to you.

PALEY
You wouldn't know it.

MURROW
Is it credit you want?

(CONTINUED)

> PALEY
> I never censored a single program,
> I hold on to affiliates who wanted
> <u>entertainment</u> from us, I've fought
> to keep our license with the same
> politicians that you were bringing
> down, and I never said no to you.
> Never.

> MURROW
> I would argue that we've done well
> by one another. I would argue
> that this network is defined by
> what the news department has
> accomplished. I would also argue
> that never saying no, is not the
> same as "not censoring."

> PALEY
> Really. Well you should teach
> journalism... You and Mr.
> Friendly.

Pause.

> PALEY (CONT'D)
> Let me ask you this: Why didn't
> you correct McCarthy when he said
> that Alger Hiss had been convicted
> of treason? He was only convicted
> of perjury. You corrected
> everything else. Did you not want
> the appearance of defending a
> known communist? I would argue
> that everyone censors... including
> you.

> MURROW
> What do you want to do, Bill?

> PALEY
> I'm going to take your show from
> half an hour to an hour. But, it
> won't be a weekly program. And,
> it won't be Tuesday night.

> MURROW
> When would it be?

> PALEY
> Sunday afternoon.

Silence.

(CONTINUED)

>           MURROW
> How many episodes?

>           PALEY
> Five.

>           MURROW
> Why don't you just fire me?

>           PALEY
> I don't think it's what either of
> us wants.

Silence.

>           PALEY (CONT'D)
> You owe me five shows.

>           MURROW
> You won't like the subject matter.

Murrow and Friendly get up to leave.

>           PALEY
> Probably not.  Fred, I'll need you
> for a moment.

We follow Murrow out to the hall where he waits for Fred.
We stay on his face for a few moments and then we hear
Fred approach.

They walk down the executive hallway.

>           FRIENDLY
> He wants me to lay a few people
> off.

>           MURROW
> I'm sure.

>           FRIENDLY
> Let's do the first show about the
> downfall of television.

>           MURROW
> The Senate's gonna vote to censure
> McCarthy tomorrow...

>           FRIENDLY
> Probably.

>           MURROW
> What happens then?

(CONTINUED)

70    CONTINUED: (4)                                    70

> FRIENDLY
> He sits in the back row...

> MURROW
> Right... they keep him in the
> Senate... they don't kick him out.

> FRIENDLY
> No... he stays... he'll just lose
> all of his power.

> MURROW
> He's already lost all his power...
> now it's just teaching him a
> lesson.

This sits with the two old friends.

They start to walk to the elevators.

> FRIENDLY
> Well, we might as well go down
> swinging. We'll do the story
> about the migrant farm workers...
> make a couple of enemies.

> MURROW
> Have you seen the latest polls
> Fred? The most trusted man in
> America is Milton Berle.

> FRIENDLY
> See, maybe you should have worn a
> dress.

> MURROW
> Works for Hoover.

> FRIENDLY
> Shhh... he's listening.

> MURROW
> How does scotch sound?

> FRIENDLY
> Scotch is good.

> MURROW
> Did you know Joe and Shirley were
> married?

> FRIENDLY
> Sure.

(CONTINUED)

70      CONTINUED: (5)                                      70

                        MURROW
            Did everybody know?

                        FRIENDLY
            Pretty much...

As Murrow and Friendly exit past camera, we slowly push
in on the two wall monitors in the lobby. Eisenhower is
giving a speech that is being broadcast on both coasts.
As he continues to talk, we get closer and closer, until
one monitor finally fills the entire frame.

                        EISENHOWER
            Why are we proud? We are proud,
            first of all because from the
            beginning of this nation, man can
            walk upright. No matter who he is
            or who she is. He can walk
            upright and meet his friend or his
            enemy. And he does not fear
            because that enemy may be a
            position in great power that he
            can be suddenly thrown in jail to
            rot there without charges and with
            no recourse to justice. We have
            the habeas corpus act and we
            respect it.

                                            DISSOLVE TO:


71      INT. CHICAGO HOTEL - BALLROOM AND THEATER - NIGHT      71

We are back to where we started. 1958, MURROW finishes
his opening address to the The Radio and Television News
Directors Association Annual meeting.

                        MURROW
            I began by saying that our history
            will be what we make it. If we go
            on as we are, then history will
            take its revenge, and retribution
            will not limp in catching up with
            us. Just once in a while, let us
            exalt the importance of ideas and
            information.
                        (MORE)


                                            (CONTINUED)

71     CONTINUED:                                                    71

MURROW (CONT'D)
Let us dream to the extent of
saying that on a given Sunday
night, the time normally occupied
by Ed Sullivan is given over to a
clinical survey on the state of
American education, and a week or
two later, the time normally used
by Steve Allen is devoted to a
thorough going study of American
policy in the Middle East.

MURROW (CONT'D)
Would the corporate image of their
respective sponsors be damaged?
Would the stockholders rise up in
their wrath and complain?  Would
anything happen other than a few
million people would have received
a little illumination on subjects
that may well determine the future
of this country and therefore the
future of the corporations?
To those who say people wouldn't
look, they wouldn't be interested,
they're too complacent,
indifferent and insulated, I can
only reply- there is, in one
reporter's opinion, considerable
evidence against that contention.
But even if they are right, what
have they got to lose?

Because if they are right, and
this instrument is good for
nothing but to entertain, amuse
and insulate, then the tube is
flickering now and we will soon
see that the whole struggle is
lost.  Otherwise, it is merely
wires and lights in a box...Good
Night.  And, Good Luck.

We fade to black.

# Cast and Crew Credits

WARNER INDEPENDENT PICTURES and 2929 ENTERTAINMENT and PARTICI-
PANT PRODUCTIONS in association with DAVIS FILMS REDBUS PICTURES and
TOHOKUSHINSHA present a SECTION EIGHT Production

## "GOOD NIGHT, AND GOOD LUCK."

DAVID STRATHAIRN    PATRICIA CLARKSON    GEORGE CLOONEY
JEFF DANIELS    ROBERT DOWNEY JR.    FRANK LANGELLA

Casting by
Ellen Chenoweth

Costume Designer
Louise Frogley

Edited by
Stephen Mirrione A.C.E.

Production Designer
Jim Bissell

Director of Photography
Robert Elswit A.S.C.

Co-Producer
Barbara A. Hall

Co-Producers
Simon Franks
Zygi Kamasa
Kiyotaka Ninomiya

Co-Executive Producers
Samuel Hadida
Victor Hadida

Executive Producers
Steven Soderbergh
Jennifer Fox
Ben Cosgrove

Executive Producers
Jeff Skoll
Chris Salvaterra

Executive Producers
Todd Wagner
Mark Cuban
Marc Butan

Produced by
Grand Heslov

Screenplay by
George Glooney & Grant
Heslov

Directed by
George Clooney

### CAST

| | |
|---|---|
| David Strathairn | Edward R. Murrow |
| Robert Downey Jr. | Joe Wershba |
| Patricia Clarkson | Shirley Wershba |
| Ray Wise | Don Hollenbeck |
| Frank Langella | William Paley |
| Jeff Daniels | Sig Mickelson |
| George Clooney | Fred Friendly |
| Tate Donovan | Jesse Zousmer |
| Tom McCarthy | Palmer Williams |
| Matt Ross | Eddie Scott |
| Reed Diamond | John Aaron |
| Robert John Burke | Charlie Mack |
| Grant Heslov | Don Hewitt |
| Alex Borstein | Natalie |
| Rose Abdoo | Millie Lerner |
| Glenn Morshower | Colonel Anderson |
| Don Creech | Colonel Jenkins |
| Helen Slayton-Hughes | Mary |
| Robert Knepper | Don Surine |
| JD Cullum | Stage Manager |
| Simon Helberg | CBS Page |
| Peter Jacobson | Jimmy |
| Dianne Reeves | Jazz Singer |

### CREW

| | |
|---|---|
| George Clooney | Director/Writer |
| Steven Soderbergh | Executive Producer |
| Grant Heslov | Producer/Writer |
| Ben Cosgrove | Executive Producer |
| Jennifer Fox | Executive Producer |
| Todd Wagner | Executive Producer |
| Mark Cuban | Executive Producer |
| Marc Butan | Executive Producer |
| Jeff Skoll | Executive Producer |
| Barbara A. Hall | Co-Producer/Unit Production Manager |
| Nicole Widmyer | Production Coordinator |

Michelle Lankwardern . . . . . . . . . . . .
Assistant Production Coordinator

Jim Bissell . . . . . . . Production Designer
Christa Munro . . . . . . . . . Art Director
Gae Buckley . . . . . . . . . Set Designer
Charlotte Raybourn . . . . . . . . . . . . .
Art Department Coordinator

David Webb . . . . . First Assistant Director
Melissa V. Barnes. . Second Assistant Director
Richard Gonzales . . . . . . . . . . . . .
Second Second Assistant Director

Robert Elswit . . . Director of Photography
Collin Anderson Camera Operator/Steadicam
Michael Pinkey . . . . . . Camera Operator
Barry "Baz" Idoine. . . . . . . . . . . . . .
"A" Camera First Assistant Camera
Larissa Supplitt . . . . . . . . . . . . . . .
"A" Camera Second Assistant Camera
John Connor. . . . . . . . . . . . . . . .
"B" Camera First Assistant Camera
Alexandra Kravetz . . . . . . . . . . . . . .
"B" Camera Second Assistant Camera

Melinda Sue Gordon . . . Still Photographer

Ellen Chenoweth . . . . . . Casting Director
Rachel Tenner . . . . . . . Casting Associate

Louise Frogley . . . . . . Costume Designer
Lynda Foote . . . . . . Costume Supervisor

Joy Zapata. . . . . . . . . . Key Hairstylist
Ron Berkeley . . . . . . . . Key Make-up

Stephen Mirrione . . . . . . . . . . Editor
Aaron Glascock . . Supervising Sound Editor
Curt Schulkey. . . Supervising Sound Editor
Allen Sviridoff. . . . . . Music Supervisor
Peter Phillips. . . . . . . . Post Supervisor
Doug Crise . . . . . . . . Assistant Editor
Matt Absher . . . . . . . . Assistant Editor

Tony Bonaventure. . . . . . . Prop Master
Ellis Barbocoff. . . . . Assistant Prop Master

Diane Newman . . . . . Script Supervisor
Jan Pascale . . . . . . . . . . Set Decorator

Edward Tise . . . . Production Sound Mixer
Randy Johnson . . . . . . Boom Operator

# Background on the
# Historical Characters

**EDWARD R. MURROW (David Strathairn)**
A legendary figure whose impact on electronic newsgathering is still felt to this day, Edward R. Murrow did not merely influence the development of broadcast journalism, he helped invent the form. His shortwave radio broadcasts from Europe in the days leading up to World War II brought a new immediacy to coverage of foreign news, his live reports from the war's frontlines made his distinctive voice universally recognizable, and his television documentaries set the standard for illustrating social and political issues by putting a human face on them. He helped shape television journalism during its infancy with his passion for the truth and his tireless efforts to advance democratic ideals, not the least of which he is frequently associated with in the mind of the public: free speech.

Murrow was born Egbert Roscoe Murrow in Polecat Creek in Guilford County, North Carolina on April 25, 1908. He grew up in a Quaker abolitionist household—one that provided him with a conscience, which would later fuel his fearless pursuit of the truth. He graduated from Washington State College in 1930 with a degree in speech and moved to New York City to work for the National Student Federation. He then served as assistant director of the Institute of International Education from 1932 to 1935, during which time he married Janet Huntington Brewster. They had one son.

In 1935, Murrow began his career at CBS as director of talks and education. Two years later, he became the director of their European

Bureau in London, where he assembled a group of reporters, including William Shirer, Charles Collingwood, Eric Sevaried, Bill Shael, and Howard K. Smith, whose reports of the war from the front lines made them popular back in the States.

After the war, Murrow returned to the United States as CBS Vice President and Director of Public Affairs, but resigned to return to radio broadcasting. With Fred Friendly, Murrow produced the series *Hear It Now* from 1950 to 1951, serving as the show's host, as well. The popularity of the show brought Murrow back to television; the team adapted their program for TV, calling it *See It Now*. The show opened with the first live simultaneous transmission from both the East Coast and the West Coast. Murrow's program on Milo Radulovich, which ultimately led to the legendary telecast focusing on Senator Joseph R. McCarthy in 1954, is considered by many as marking the turning point not only in the senator's campaign against Communist sympathizers but in the history of television, as well.

During the same time period, Murrow hosted *Person to Person*, which featured informal chats with celebrities such as Marilyn Monroe and John Steinbeck. While less controversial, the show and its format continue to influence today's celebrity interviewers. He continued with that program for a year after *See It Now* ended in 1958, the same year Murrow began moderating and producing *Small World*—another innovative program, featuring discussions among international political figures.

Murrow won five Emmys and five Peabody Awards for his work, and he continued to demand more from himself and his colleagues over the years, as demonstrated by a speech he gave at the Radio and Television News Directors Association convention in 1958. "This just might do nobody any good," the speech began grimly, and Murrow went on to describe the untenable position of the journalist broadcasting on instruments whose development had been shaped by—and would continue to grow as—an impossible combination of news, show business, and advertising. Murrow mentioned his employer only a few times in his speech, but it was clear that he included CBS in his criticism of the networks and the effect their unchecked competition for ratings had on news programs.

He left CBS in 1961 when he was appointed by President John F. Kennedy to head the U.S. Information Agency, a post he remained at until 1964.

Murrow died of lung cancer in New York on April 27, 1965.

## SEE IT NOW

Network television's first newsmagazine, *See It Now* aired on CBS for six years, starting in 1951, and quickly set a standard for televised news and journalism as a whole. Born from the Murrow/Friendly–produced CBS radio show *Hear It Now*, *See It Now* did more than just report the news; it engaged in intellectual discussions and analysis of the issues of the day, oftentimes leading into political and social commentaries. Murrow and his team covered hot topics, often political in nature, ranging from life in the nuclear age to our country's calls to war. Reporting the anti-Communist rage sweeping the nation required more delicate dealings, and in October 1953, *See It Now* found and aired an episode focusing on Senator McCarthy. That led to two more in 1954 exposing McCarthy's tyrannical behavior and putting an end to his witch hunt of Communists. *See It Now* continued to air as specials until 1957, though as a result of its most provocative and groundbreaking broadcasts involving McCarthy, those that followed were relatively tame in tone.

## FRED FRIENDLY (George Clooney)

Fred Friendly co-produced *See It Now* alongside Edward R. Murrow. Their partnership started in a series of records covering news stories from the war front, *I Can Hear It Now*. They adapted these into a radio show, *Hear It Now*, which became the basis for network television's first newsmagazine show, *See It Now*. Friendly went on to become the president of the CBS News Division in 1964, but resigned two years later after disagreeing with the network's decision to air an *I Love Lucy* rerun instead of broadcasting live coverage of the Senate's hearings on America's involvement in Vietnam. Upon leaving CBS, Friendly took the Edward R. Murrow seat as a professor of journalism at Columbia University. Throughout his distinguished career, Friendly received a total of ten Peabody Awards.

## DON HEWITT (Grant Heslov)

Don Hewitt directed *See It Now*, which first aired in 1951. He has spent his entire career at CBS. In addition to producing and directing the first-ever televised presidential debate, in 1960, he produced and directed the inaugural year of the *CBS Evening News with Walter Cronkite* in 1963, and created *60 Minutes*, which premiered in 1968. CBS notes that between September 1968 and 2003, there have been over three thousand original stories on *60 Minutes*, nearly every one of which has had to meet with Hewitt's approval.

## SIGFRIED "SIG" MICKELSON (Jeff Daniels)

Sig Mickelson, head of the CBS Network News and Public Affairs division, helped develop the format of *Hear It Now* with Fred Friendly in anticipation of shaping it into *See It Now*. Abandoning the reliance on newsreel companies, Mickelson was instrumental in building an in-house department of camera crews to document footage.

## WILLIAM S. PALEY (Frank Langella)

William S. Paley ran the CBS radio and television networks for more than half a century. He served as president of the network until 1946, when he became chairman of the CBS Board. Paley established the radio network's first programming department in the late 1940s, and went on to promote the development of the news division, which gave birth to *See It Now* in 1951. Paley retained his chairmanship of CBS until his death in 1990. His was the primary donation in 1976 that helped create what is now the Museum of Television and Radio in New York City.

## JOE WERSHBA (Robert Downey Jr.)

Joe Wershba started his career in radio before moving into television journalism. A producer on *See It Now*, he captured the Milo J. Radulovich footage and was part of the team that broadcast the brave shows challenging Senator Joseph McCarthy. Wershba continued to work at CBS and became one of the original producers of *60 Minutes* alongside Don Hewitt. After retiring, Wershba worked on film documentaries in the United States and Asia, and contributed to Walter Cronkite's memoirs. He is the recipient of the highly prized Silurian award for lifetime excellence in journalism and has been nominated for a Pulitzer Prize, in addition to receiving two Emmy awards.

### SHIRLEY WERSHBA (Patricia Clarkson)
Shirley Wershba helped develop one of the first radio shows devoted to women's issues, *Dimension of a Woman's World*. Married to Joseph Wershba, the two had to keep their marriage secret due to network rules. In 1965, her focus returned to television and she contributed to *CBS News*, *ABC Evening News with Peter Jennings*, and as producer-writer on the *Morning News* for CBS. In 1975, she was one of the three original producers of the *MacNeil/Lehrer Report* on PBS and also produced for *60 Minutes*. In 1983, she was nominated for an Emmy for producing Diane Sawyer's *Morning News* interview with Richard Nixon.

### SENATOR JOSEPH P. McCARTHY
As a Senator in the post–World War II era, McCarthy devoted much time to exposing subversives (Communists or their sympathizers), a mission sparked when he claimed to have a list of such subversives working in the State Department. For this, or any of his accusations, McCarthy failed to ever provide hard evidence. In early 1954, McCarthy's hearings of accused subversives were broadcast, the first televised hearings ever. *See It Now* reported on these hearings and the misuse and abuse of legislative power on the part of the Senator. The program allowed a rebuttal from the junior senator, whose appearance on *See It Now* exposed McCarthy's tyrannical, one-sided motivations, leading to his being censured by the Senate.

### LIEUTENANT MILO RADULOVICH
Born in the United States to immigrant parents, Milo Radulovich was a World War II veteran working as a meteorologist and an Air Force reservist with top-secret clearance. In 1953, Radulovich was served with discharge papers, having been deemed a security risk because his father and sister were supposedly Communist sympathizers.

He was stripped of his commission after losing his first court case. Murrow read about Radulovich's experiences and found his the ideal story to expose Senator McCarthy and his witch hunt. *See It Now* aired Radulovich's story on October 20, 1953, and one month later he was reinstated to the military. After a career as a meteorologist with the National Weather Service, Radulovich retired and now lives in Lodi, California.

# About the Co-Writers

**GEORGE CLOONEY (Director / Co-Writer / "Fred Friendly")**
Partnered with Steven Soderbergh in the film and television production company Section Eight, they have produced *Ocean's Twelve*, *Ocean's Eleven, Confessions of a Dangerous Mind, The Jacket, Full Frontal*, and *Welcome to Collinwood*. He was also an executive producer for two critically acclaimed Section Eight films, Warner Bros.' *Insomnia* and Focus Features' *Far from Heaven*.

George Clooney made his directorial debut in 2002 with *Confessions of a Dangerous Mind* (Miramax), for which he won the Special Achievement in Film award from the National Board of Review. He also works with Section Eight television division. He was an executive producer and directed five episodes of *Unscripted*, a reality-based show that debuted on HBO in January. He also was an executive producer and cameraman for *K Street*, also for HBO.

Clooney starred in the blockbuster hits *Ocean's Twelve* and *Ocean's Eleven*. He also starred in the Coen brothers' *O Brother, Where Art Thou?* and won the 2000 Golden Globe Award as Best Actor in a Motion Picture Musical or Comedy. He earned critical acclaim in the award-winning drama *Three Kings* and in the Oscar-nominated *Out of Sight*. His previous feature films include *The Peacemaker, Batman & Robin, One Fine Day* and *From Dusk Till Dawn*.

Prior to playing lead roles in blockbuster features, Clooney starred in several television series but is perhaps best known to TV audiences for his five years on the hit NBC drama *ER*. His portrayal of Dr. Douglas Ross earned him Golden Globe, Screen Actors Guild, People's Choice and Emmy nominations.

Clooney was executive producer and co-star of the live television broadcast of *Fail Safe,* an Emmy-winning telefilm developed through his Maysville Pictures and based on the '60s novel of the same name. In 2000, it was nominated for a Golden Globe Award as Best Mini-series or Motion Picture Made for Television.

Section Eight has produced Clooney's next two projects: *Syriana* and *The Good German.* In *Syriana,* Clooney plays a CIA agent who fights terrorism, and also serves as one of the film's producers. *The Good German* started production in September 2005.

### GRANT HESLOV (Producer / Co-Writer / "Don Hewitt")

Grant Heslov is president of Section Eight Television, George Clooney and Steven Soderbergh's Warner Bros.–based production company. He also directed the feature film *Par 6* and the short *Waiting for Woody.*

Along with his producing and directing, Heslov has had a long career as an actor. Some of his TV credits include CBS's *CSI: Crime Scene Investigation* and Fox's *The X-Files.* Some of his feature credits include roles in *The Scorpion King* starring Duane "the Rock" Johnson, *Enemy of the State* starring Will Smith, *Dante's Peak* starring Pierce Brosnan, *The Birdcage* starring Robin Williams, Michael Crichton's *Congo* and James Cameron's *True Lies* starring Arnold Schwarzenegger.

Heslov served as director and producer of the critically acclaimed series *Unscripted,* and co-executive producer of *K Street,* both for HBO. He is currently developing a ten-part series based on the Ten Commandments, with installments to be directed by Soderbergh and Clooney, among others.